What Happens in Management

WHAT HAPPENS IN MANAGEMENT

Principles
and
Practices

MAURICE R. HECHT

A Division of
American Management Associations

62025

Library of Congress Cataloging in Publication Data

Hecht, Maurice R
  What happens in management.

  Includes index.
  1. Management. 2. Organization. I. Title.
HD31.H398   658   79-54835
ISBN 0-8144-5586-7

© 1980 AMACOM
A division of American Management Associations, New York.
All rights reserved. Printed in the United States of America.

First Printing

To
Mary

Preface

Many personal experiences, as well as information gathered over the years from friends in a wide variety of businesses and several universities, have gone into this book. The original sources of some of the concepts used here go back a long time, and I trust that I have not inadvertently stepped on anyone's toes. I have tried to put together a description of what happens in management, providing enough information to make an understandable story. I have not attempted to include everybody's ideas on a variety of topics, but have only used those which I find most useful to the understanding of a practical manager.

This book is intended to be a practical one. Theories have been conscientiously used but have been put in the background, because I do not feel that a manager has to have a full understanding of history and a knowledge of all theories in order to be a skillful practitioner. The basic ideas of this book have been filtered through my own experiences in the work world as well as through countless discussions with working managers. I do hope that they prove useful.

Maurice R. Hecht

Contents

CHAPTER 1

Management

What is management?

A simple enough question, but there is no simple answer. Many a person who carries the title of manager is not really a manager. Open a dozen textbooks and you will find a variety of answers. Some books never define the word, some define it so rigidly that you could almost make one in a machine shop. A common statement is that a manager is a person who gets work done through people. Such a person could be a slave gang boss or a tricky manipulator, bending people somehow to do his bidding. And again he could be a manager.

To approach some definition, let us say that a manager is a person charged with, or assuming charge of, a number of people working at the task of getting some activity accomplished within a set period of time. The result could be a physical product or a service. The manager works with others to reach the objective. He may do none of the actual work himself but see that the work is accomplished by those who work for him.

The manager may personally contribute to the work. For example, the head of a drafting department may apply his personal abilities to solve some technical problem being experienced. He may also support those working for him. Thus a sales manager may call on a major client, not to do the direct selling but to help out his sales representative.

Some people distinguish managers from what they call administrators, with the administrators being those who set policies and coordinate activities at the top. These could be senior men and even active board members. All those below occupied in managerial work are called managers. We will make no such distinction in this book. We will talk about levels of management but will not include board members. After all, stockholders should set general policies through the board as politicians, acting presumably in the name of the people, set policies for those working in government ranks.

Having said all this, we still have more to say to get some view of what a manager is, what he does, and how he does it.

A manager works in an organization—be it a business or a government or social agency—that sets out to accomplish some objectives. In view of this overall mission of the organization, the structure of its management is that of an accountability system predicated on human judgment. Managers are workers in this organization, even though they're not turning metal, making sales calls, doing counseling work, or putting financial figures into a machine. At the lower levels, managers have to have other people, as well as equipment, doing the required jobs; at a higher level, they coordinate the work of other managers.

MINIMUM RESPONSIBILITIES OF A MANAGER

To be accountable for his part of the organization's work at any level, a manager requires four minimal conditions:

1. The right to hire any person working for him or at least to say whether he wishes to have a person sent to work for him.

2. The right to decide the work to be done by his workers.
3. The right to judge the performance of his workers and award them accordingly.
4. The right to dismiss a person working for him or, if the outfit is large enough, have him transferred to another part of the organization where he may fit in.

Managers are naturally working within ground rules set by the organization and not going off as they please. Workers would have the right to appeal, particularly to their manager's manager or to a grievance committee.

It is these four basic conditions which set off the managers from the nonmanagers, whatever titles or names are actually applied to them. Without these conditions, no manager can be held accountable for getting his share of the work done.

To accomplish his work, a manager needs certain competencies. Basically, they are the skills required in his work, a clear understanding of what he is supposed to accomplish (vision may be a glorified way of saying this), and the ability to communicate with people and give them the leadership required to get the work accomplished.

AN ART AND A SCIENCE

Management is an art and a science. Science sets parameters, provides focus, and eliminates the poorest decisions; but when all the figures are in and thought about, intuition, whatever we might call it, makes the final decisions. This is true at the high levels as well as those below.

Obtaining facts and figures, aside from providing quantitative guidelines, is essential because studying them stimulates the knowledge beneath the surface of every person and brings it to aid in making the final decisions. If logical methods are not used at all, then relying on intuition is just playing lady luck. This is not the role for a good manager; he may and should take calculated risks, but not be a gambler. Who would wish to drive with a person who drove only by intuition and had no driving skills? A trained driver who practices his skills and is also a defensive driver is generally a much more capable one.

In a 1974 lecture to the Oxford Centre for Management Studies at Oxford University entitled "Is Management Really an Art?" (reprinted in the *Harvard Business Review,* January–February 1975), Henry M. Boettinger took a look at great artists in several fields, from painting to ballet, and discovered that artists who were top performers had at least two good qualities: great technical competence and imagination. Boettinger noted that these were also the qualities of a good manager, for he is one who knows his craft, is imaginative about it, and can communicate his feelings to those who work for him. So much for artists who despise craftsmanship or managers who won't acquire competency. And there are plenty of both around!

The competencies that must be acquired by every manager are the ability to handle the functions of management and to deal effectively with people to get the work done.

The reference to functions is not to such things as marketing, finance, manufacturing, and so on. These are the functions of the organization, as opposed to the functions of management. Unfortunately various people use different names to describe management functions. Here we will stick to five simple ones that are commonly used. They are planning, organizing, staffing, directing, and controlling.

A BROAD LOOK AT MANAGEMENT

We will start off with a broad look at management and then zoom in on various areas for deeper looks. Management is an activity, and if you start by looking at little pieces here and there, you can destroy the understanding of the whole. However, we will have to look at certain chunks, since the whole subject is too complex to discuss at once in any depth. As we do this, bear in mind that there is a living relationship between the chunks and that they cannot simply be put together like stones to construct a wall. They are more like parts of a body, which you can study separately up to a point but can't simply throw together to make a living creature. There are management ideas common to all management jobs. Experience in one field of activity may be helpful to a person who stays in that field and may make him a better manager than a person with no background in that field; however, it does not indicate that he has the capacity to undertake a higher position. A highly capable manager from outside is often a great asset to an organization.

Socrates, the Greek philosopher, stated this idea clearly some 2,000 years ago in a discussion he is reputed to have had with Nicomachides, who had tried to obtain a senior post in the army but had lost out to the merchant Antisthenes. During the conversation, Socrates reminded Nicomachides that Antisthenes had been very successful in organizing choruses. When Nicomachides objected that he couldn't see any similarity between managing a chorus and managing an army, Socrates reminded him that Antisthenes had had no skill in music or choral conducting before taking on that job but that the merchant had gotten the best people in the field to do the work. If he could have done this with music, the philosopher asked his friend, why couldn't he apply the same principles to running an army? According to Socrates, the most important thing is to have a clear idea of what is needed and then to provide it—for a chorus, an army, or an entire city.

FOLKLORE AND REALITY

There is much folklore about management which doesn't always fit reality, such as the myth that the organization chart shows how an organization works. Although such a chart should be drawn up to show the broad picture and the general lines of authority, it does not and cannot show the flesh and blood of an organization in action, nor is it meant to do that.

A related myth has it that the many and varied tools of management are the substance of management itself. It states that to utilize any tool from work study to job enrichment to systems technology makes one a good manager. They are needed tools, but they do not make a person a good manager anymore than a good hammer and saw make one a good furniture maker. They may make one a good rough carpenter, but that is all. The tools of management come after the essence of management—the planning to achieve objectives, the decisions on what should be done, the working with people to coordinate and accomplish results. The tools come into use when the substance is understood, and then they help tackle the problems better and should improve the output of the organization, be it product or service. That is, the question "What are we trying to do?" must be addressed before the question "How do we do it?" Experience generally helps with the first.

Another myth states that a driving superman full of sizzle and always on the go is the trademark of an excellent manager. It is often the trademark of a man who spreads chaos and disarray rather than provides good leadership. Senior managers sometimes fall prey to this misconception and think of themselves as wartime commanders leading their troops to victory in a struggle to save the motherland or the fatherland or what have you. They fail to realize that all employees are not motivated in the same way as they are, that we are not brothers or sisters under the skin. Their style is often seen as that of a driving maniac whose perceptions of reality are out of line with the views of those who slave for him. Most managers actually lead more normal lives and generally take time off.

Professor Henry Mintzberg of McGill University points out a number of additional myths about management in his book *The Nature of Managerial Work.** A first fiction, he states, is that the manager is a reflective and systematic planner. In fact, Mintzberg says, the evidence is that managers work at a tough pace but their activities are generally brief, discontinuous, and varied. They tend to prefer action to thought.

A second myth often perpetuated in many textbooks is that the manager has no regular duties to perform. Mintzberg points out that there are numerous regular duties, often of a ritualistic nature

*New York: Harper & Row, 1973.

(for example, the sales manager or president may regularly visit big customers). A key duty is the gathering of soft information and placing it into the mainstream of the organization's thinking. Often a senior manager hears news and comments that others lower down do not hear. This information can be very useful to the organization.

A third piece of folklore is that a senior manager requires total organized information. Great emphasis was placed in past years (and still is) on developing management tools of grandiose proportions into Management Information Systems. A manager could look at these from his perch high up in the work hierarchy and nod "yes" or "no," similar to a Roman emperor giving thumbs up or down to a gladiator after a fight. Mintzberg points out that this myth is not true; most managers favor meetings and telephone calls and not fat collations of computer information. There is a time for such systematic studies, but managers do not stick to them as their main or only source of learning what's going on.

A final myth listed by Mintzberg is that management is fast becoming a science and a profession. We dealt a bit with this previously in noting the study made by Henry Boettinger. Mintzberg adds that the managers' programs, which consist of scheduling time, processing information, making decisions, and other activities, are locked deep inside their brains. Judgment and intuition come strongly into play. This observation is similar to our note that the work setup of an organization is an accountability system dependent on human judgment.

These myths and realities are cited here not to discourage people from learning about management but (1) to cut away the false folklore about what a manager is, (2) to prevent people from merely learning skills and tools and thinking that *that* is management, and (3) to bring some clarity to the fact that a good manager is not a living computer that can be programmed with tools and skills but a skillful human who works just enough structure into any situation to get tasks accomplished.

If this is understood, then what a person has to do is recall whatever life experiences can help him manage, and learn in the following pages a variety of knowledge and skills that can aid him in this task.

THE NATURE OF HUMAN WORK

What is the nature of human work? The answer to this question is important to anyone who wishes to manage the work activities of people.

Work, especially when we are measuring it, is commonly thought of in simple physical terms. The physicists think of work as the movement of mass through space, and that is how they measure it. For their purposes the definition is fine, but human work has more than a physical dimension. Often, too, when we think of work, we think of it in overly specific terms—say, shaping steel to certain specifications or extolling the pluses of a motor car to would-be buyers. We will look at this more critically when we come to discuss dividing up work and creating organizations.

For now our purpose is to demonstrate the dual aspects of human work. The word "work" itself and, to a lesser extent, the word management have been so accepted as part of human activities that neither has been carefully analyzed to see what is actually meant by them. If work were strictly a mechanical activity, then some day all work will be mechanized or computerized or both, and men will have little to do. But human work is more than this.

Human work is a goal-directed activity with two major characteristics. One, it requires knowledge (including skills) so that it can be carried out within set-down limits, including material limitations, various policies, rules, and regulations, limits of time and money. Two, it involves an element of essential uncertainty concerning the use of personal discretion in carrying it out.

The first aspect is subject to automation and computerization; the second one is not. Uncertainty is an unavoidable psychological aspect of work. It exists in the minds of all working people, not only those at high levels. To the extent that tasks can be mechanized at lower levels, uncertainty can be eliminated; but as long as the work is performed by a human being, this basic psychological aspect of work is personally felt. From a workman using a drill and mentally adjusting himself to the jigs used in making his holes to the senior executive projecting years ahead to share in a business market, uncertainty is an important ingredient of work. Both are concerned with whether they are performing well, and they remain in a state of uncertainty for some time.

At the lowest level, the time span of uncertainty or psychological concern over what one is doing may be extremely limited. A clerk filing material decides to open a new file as he thinks this should be done. He soon finds out from a supervisor if he has done the right thing. Thus the span of time involved in using his personal discretion is very short. As you go up the management scale, the time of uncertainty may be years, particularly if extensive research and product and market testing must be done before management knows if it is right or wrong. Somebody who can't work at his own discretion over a long period of time could never handle a senior management position.

No one knows for sure what it takes to be a good manager. The basic requirement appears to be a mixture of intelligence, knowledge, skills and competencies, initiative, and motivation to achieve. Insofar as intelligence and motivation cannot be learned, the study of management should focus on the skills, knowledge, and competencies required to carry out with others goal-directed activities with objectives to be met. This requires not only a knowledge of man and why he behaves as he does—that is, how he is motivated and behaves under different conditions—but how to plan, organize, staff, direct, and control an organization in which people and activities are coordinated to achieve desired results.

In any organization people perform duties that are related to each other. The manner in which these duties interrelate and the behavioral rules which guide people, as well as the activities or tasks to be performed and the atmosphere in which performances take place, all are vital to understanding management. This is the main reason why we will spend about equal amounts of time in this book on studying people as human beings and on examining the structure and operation of the organizations in which people work. The material on the next two pages will help managers to evaluate their interpersonal skills at the work place.

Questions for Managers (and Would-Be Ones) to Ask Themselves

1. Do I like being accountable for the activities of others?
2. Do I like explaining clearly and frankly to my superiors what I am doing?
3. Do I have empathy, that is, do I have a clear perception of people, their desires, their fears?
4. Can I deal with people without showing annoyance and dislike sometimes?
5. Can I direct my subordinates and give them proper leadership?
6. Do I keep my activities within reasonable time units?
7. Can I see problems ahead and act to prevent them from becoming serious?
8. Do I tend generally to check out items first and not make snap decisions?
9. Do I listen to people without jumping in quickly?
10. Do I give people proper attention when they bring matters up?
11. Do I create a climate where people can freely open up with their own ideas?
12. Do I hear clearly what people are saying?
13. Do I tend to keep my cool when my ideas are criticized by my subordinates?
14. Can I take criticism from my superiors?
15. Do I praise my subordinates when they do a good job?
16. Do I fully realize that I will not accomplish my objectives unless my subordinates accomplish theirs?
17. Do I avoid showing favoritism in my work group?
18. Do I feel good when I see my subordinates succeeding?
19. Do I understand that I have to exercise control over my subordinates?
20. Can I carry out company policies I may not fully agree with without making senior people the scapegoats so the heat is off me?
21. Can I accomplish objectives within budget and time limitations?
22. Have I new ideas to bring regularly to my work?
23. Do I try to keep abreast of my work by reading and going to seminars or other similar activities from time to time?
24. Do I enjoy one-to-one or small group sessions where I can counsel people and help them improve their work without acting like a bossy school teacher?
25. Do I make long-term plans (one year or more to complete objectives) and work at them patiently without quitting them?

To evaluate yourself on these questions, tick off your responses as honestly as you can on the chart below in order to give yourself a realistic opinion. Get a subtotal by adding the number of checks in each column; then multiply by the number given. Add these figures for a grand total, and rate yourself according to the scale shown at the bottom of the chart.

Question	Always	Quite Often	Often	Rarely	Never
1.	_____	_____	_____	_____	_____
2.	_____	_____	_____	_____	_____
3.	_____	_____	_____	_____	_____
4.	_____	_____	_____	_____	_____
5.	_____	_____	_____	_____	_____
6.	_____	_____	_____	_____	_____
7.	_____	_____	_____	_____	_____
8.	_____	_____	_____	_____	_____
9.	_____	_____	_____	_____	_____
10.	_____	_____	_____	_____	_____
11.	_____	_____	_____	_____	_____
12.	_____	_____	_____	_____	_____
13.	_____	_____	_____	_____	_____
14.	_____	_____	_____	_____	_____
15.	_____	_____	_____	_____	_____
16.	_____	_____	_____	_____	_____
17.	_____	_____	_____	_____	_____
18.	_____	_____	_____	_____	_____
19.	_____	_____	_____	_____	_____
20.	_____	_____	_____	_____	_____
21.	_____	_____	_____	_____	_____
22.	_____	_____	_____	_____	_____
23.	_____	_____	_____	_____	_____
24.	_____	_____	_____	_____	_____
25.	_____	_____	_____	_____	_____
Subtotal					
	× 4	× 3	× 2	× 1	0
Total	_____ +	_____ +	_____ +	_____ =	_____

Rating Scale: 80–100, very good; 60–80, good; 40–60, think again about wanting to be a manager; below 40, try some other line of work.

Case Study
Eclipse Machinery and Electronics, Inc.

The following case, which is based on a real-life situation, involves many basic management activities and problems. Read through it once or twice, then write down your opinions of the situation using the questions at the end of the case as a guide. There is no need to stay with those questions only; if you have other comments and questions, write them down as well. It may also be useful to sketch out the relationships in the firm to obtain a rough idea of its structure and basic operating policies or lack of them.

This firm has a staff of some 125 people in the shop, office, and sales force. Charles Magneton started it when he was in his early thirties, about 12 years ago. Magneton was a graduate engineer with a flare for new ideas and little desire to work for others. When he graduated from the university 15 years ago, he went to work for a large electronics firm. He started out in sales but later became involved in shop operations. He wanted to try out many new ideas that involved broader areas than electronics. But his manager did not see eye to eye with him, and neither did the other top people, so Magneton quit and a little later started his own firm—Eclipse Machinery and Electronics.

His first customers were people he knew. He found that he was able to sell them new ideas, which he then had to develop in his shop. His first job was a small operation for an automotive parts manufacturer. He not only developed the required electronic controls but also built the moveable metals parts required in the operation. This mixture of mechanical and electronic parts fascinated him.

His own father and his wife's father, who were both relatively well off, lent him money to get started and soon things were going well for him. But Magneton quickly discovered that his plant could be very busy at times but slow at other times. He decided to take on several standard items that he could produce all the time, so that he could keep those who worked for him busy regularly.

A few engineers he had known at the university and at the plant where he first worked were attracted to his operations. Some of them had ideas on their own and soon several of them were working with him to produce special products. As time went on they kept up with developments in their field and introduced computer controls where they felt these were feasible and within costs.

In earlier days Magneton had difficulties deciding how long it would take to develop new ideas, and the firm once lost quite a bit of money on a project that took two years to complete. Magneton decided that although he enjoyed working on this project, some of his men were tired of it after a while and that the firm did not have enough capital to pursue such projects. In a meeting with them, Magneton decided that they should stick to short-term projects lasting no longer than a few months or so, with the odd one possibly going over a year. One of his better salesmen quit a while later because he wasn't happy with the decision. But Magneton has managed to keep four of the others for the last few years, and he has alternated the longer projects among them.

Originally Magneton felt that the standard product lines would be sold by his specialist salesmen while they were doing other things. This did happen at times, but he soon discovered that he had to hire salespeople who devoted all their time to the standard products. At first, Magneton had tried to select trained engineers who could do both jobs but not long afterwards found himself hiring less-trained individuals. The men selling standard products were happier doing just that, and when they came across a possibility for a special product they brought in one of the specialist salespeople and split the commission.

Eventually Magneton found that he had basically two types of salespeople (and in the standard products field, too): some liked to phone customers and get repeats on orders; others preferred to travel around the territory and get new business as well as following up on old customers. In this second group, a few actively pushed to get new customers. Magneton examined the problem and he found that there was a pattern in the amount of time various salespeople would spend on this kind of work. Only one man spent more than a few months trying to get new customers—most stayed with old ones and referrals.

Magneton found it hard to understand such people. He liked

nothing better than to go out on the road and develop new business for his firm. In fact, he was both the best technical brain in the firm and the best salesman it had. He once added up his time outside the plant and discovered that he was away about half of each working year making contacts and meeting potential clients at industrial shows and conferences and in social activities. Often he would open the door for his salespeople and check on what was happening from time to time.

When he got back from a long trip, he found that he practically had to live at the plant for the next few days because so many questions and problems had come up. He did have someone managing the shop but when each specialist sold some new ideas, he liked to follow it through the shop and push to get it completed. The supervisors and technicians in the plant tried to please these star salesmen, as they were known. When they turned to Reyburn Blooming—the shop manager—for help, he found that when he made a decision, one of these salesmen would come in later and get things changed. Magneton had to deal with all these problems when he came back.

Magneton knew that he needed more order and organization in the shop but felt that unless he stuck to his selling, there would be little need for order—since there would be no business! He hired a man named Charles Hinton to help solve some of these problems. Although not a full-fledged accountant, Hinton knew a lot about keeping books and about general office procedures.

Hinton did develop some procedures for use in the company, and Magneton was quite pleased with them. They appeared to be putting some order into the operation, and he would often discuss with Hinton some of his other ideas about the firm. Hinton gradually became involved with other activities and when Magneton was away, the production manager in particular would ask for his advice. The man who ran the warehouse and was responsible for shipping out the products also consulted him. Hinton gave his opinions, although Magneton had rarely discussed the specifics with him and had not asked him to be responsible for what happened when he was away. But Hinton did not know what else to do when asked for his opinion, since everybody knew that he was the one who discussed shop and office operations with Magneton more often than anyone else.

When Magneton came back he would often be critical of the decisions made by Hinton in his absence. But since Magneton was usually busy looking over technical matters as well as trying to read the records of his general product salesmen, he never got very mad. At first Hinton was upset by Magneton's comments, because he had developed some things which he felt were successful and of which Magneton would later voice his approval.

Hinton had once spent about four months developing an inventory control system for the warehouse, because things had been handled haphazardly there. After studying the situation and seeing what happened elsewhere, Hinton introduced a tab setup. These tabs were kept beside each product in the warehouse, and as each shipping clerk removed some of the items to send out to a customer, he noted this on the tab. Magneton said he was pleased that they now had better control, although several problems did crop up. One was that clerks sometimes misplaced tabs or forgot to return them. Another was that when there were not enough items for a customer, there was no decent back-order system. Delivery slips denoted the missing amounts but at the time stock was replenished, generally by reordering, the person who did the purchasing was not aware of accounting records of back orders. The result was a small crisis from time to time.

When these problems surfaced, Magneton asked Hinton to look into the possibilities of a computer-controlled inventory system. He suggested that Hinton talk about the idea to John Chivers, a specialist salesman, but he did not wish Hinton to take up too much of Chivers's time. Hinton got into the matter but after working on it for five months, he got tired of it and dropped it. When Magneton asked him some six months later how the project was coming, Hinton said that he did not have enough time to work on it but that he had it in mind and was doing a bit of checking from time to time. Magneton did not pursue the matter, since the firm was growing quickly and he had many other things on his mind.

Another time Magneton suggested to Hinton that they required more control of costs as special products went through the shop. He thought that they should have a special budget form to follow works in progress, and he suggested that Hinton get closer to shop operations so that such a form could be developed. This time Hinton told Magneton that he would like to do it, but that he didn't have much spare time. He asked Magneton what duties he should give up for a time and when these forms were needed. Magneton thought about it, but since he had other projects on his mind, he told Hinton to get around to doing it when there was time. "Try to do something later on," was the way he put it—then he dashed off.

Several months later Magneton did refer to the forms again. Hinton told him that he hadn't gotten around to doing them yet. Magneton was very upset, both with himself and with Hinton. He knew that the growth of the firm could not stand the current disorder for very long. He could see the waste even when he walked through the plant—and especially when he looked at the records that were being kept. He knew that when the firm was smaller, projects were carried out more efficiently. He looked over the figures for a special piece of machinery they had recently completed. The machine was very much like something they had produced a few years before, which he well remembered, for he had worked very hard on it as a new project. The figures showed that both costs and time had more than doubled. He knew that costs had gone up since then, but a lot of the basic ideas had already been worked out—he had discussed them himself with the salesman who was working on this project.

Now, Magneton was mad. He looked over other records, and the same problem was apparent. He knew he had to do something or he would face bankruptcy soon. Hinton had just not worked out as he had been expected to. Yet Magneton blamed himself as much as Hinton for this failure. He felt that the first thing he should do to get his operation straightened out was to fire Hinton and hire a real professional. He looked out of his office door into the hallway to see if Hinton were around. He saw Hinton turning a corner and moving toward the shipping department with a sheaf of papers. A clerk at the sales desk stopped him and asked him a question. Magneton saw Hinton reply something, then rush off.

Magneton was all set to follow Hinton and, in the corner of the plant where there was only scrap—too much of it—fire Hinton, throw *him* on the scrapheap. But the thought made him sick at heart. He would have to think out what he should do.

Here are some guide questions:

1. What are the general problems?
2. What are key specific problems?
3. How would you set about tackling the problems? Can you suggest some order of priorities?

CHAPTER 2

Human Aspects

In the days of slavery and serfdom it was relatively easy for the masters of the times to deal with people. They simply ignored people as human beings and treated them as they treated mechanical objects. They had jobs to do and, like pieces of wood, were expendable after serving their purpose for some time. Fortunately, those days have passed. The revolts of our ancestors have advanced us to our more democratic society. Although slavery techniques have been used in modern times, as in totalitarian states, they are unacceptable in our Western societies today.

DETERMINANTS OF HUMAN BEHAVIOR

When people cannot be treated as objects or pieces of machinery, a perennial problem remains. This is the problem in modern organizations of how to get the best work out of people so that both the individuals and the organization benefit. To do this we require answers to such questions as:

- Why do people behave as they do?
- How can I get people to respond as I want them to?
- Why don't people understand things which I think are quite simple and very clear?
- Why do people appear to act against their own best interests at times?
- Why do people respond one way in a certain situation yet another way under what seem to be similar circumstances?

What are the determinants of human behavior? Clearly a manager has to have or build up some understanding of people. He shouldn't proceed as if this information were obvious or irrelevant. Just as a marketing man would never tackle a marketing problem without some understanding of the market he was dealing with, the manager must try to understand people and their behavior.

Most managers tackle the tricky people problem without real, explicit knowledge of why people behave as they do, but unfortunately with many assumptions about people's behavior. They obtain this information by the filter method of personal experience, including reading, without testing their ideas. We all tend to look for affirmation of our ideas and are pleased when this happens. We tend to forget when we were wrong, hide it away, rationalize it. So we are left mainly with positive affirmations of our assumptions and/or prejudices. And unfortunately, this very attitude reinforces our thinking, for people's reactions to us are determined partly by what they perceive are our assumptions about them.

Three Men and a Car

Let us examine three men in a situation where they are thinking of purchasing a new car.

The first situation involves Arthur Adams and his wife. They were planning to take an extended camping trip as well as visit some relatives in a few cities. "The car is five years old, Arthur," cautioned Mrs. Adams. "How do you think it will stand the trip? Or should we think of getting a new car?"

"There is only one way to find out," replied Mr. Adams, "and that is to make a proper comparison of costs."

With that he set to work. He discovered that he could obtain about $1,000 for his car and that depreciation over the next year would be $250. Knowing the car, he estimated probable repair cost as well as the costs of insurance, gas, and oil. Then he looked into the type of new car that he would consider buying. The price shook him up a bit, but he put it down nonetheless. He thought of possible repairs that wouldn't be covered by warranty, the depreciation on the new car in the first year, the cost of gas and oil, which would be less in the new car, and all other facts.

Mr. Adams then totaled the figures for both cars and estimated that it would be $250 cheaper to hold on to his old car. He knew that he did not have a fully accurate figure by any means, but he had what he needed to make his decision.

Barry Bevans was also thinking about buying a new car. His friend and coworker Charlie Smith had come to the office in a new fancy car just recently, and that had set Bevans's brain thinking. Smith lived in a bigger house, too, and was also a member of an exclusive country club that Bevans would have liked to belong to. Charlie sure comes across as a winner, reflected Bevans, and yet he can't be making much more than I do. That very day when he thought this way, he came across an ad for a new car in the paper. It was for the new Moderne, a plush, diesel, front-wheel-drive car destined for "those who know the truth about tomorrow." And Bevans made up his mind.

Our third man, Cedric Craven, would also like to buy a new car. The old one was due for repairs now, and at the age of the car, the bill could be very high. Craven was also beginning to feel bothered that every time he took off when a light turned green, he was the last to pick up speed. His neighbors had bought a new car recently, and it looked pretty good.

However, Craven had other things to think about. Mrs. Craven wanted some new furniture for the house, and they did need a new living room set, at least. She also suggested that they should finish their unfinished recreation room, because the children were growing up and it would be nice to have them bring their friends there.

Craven complained about the slowness of the car and brought up the fact that their good friends down the street just purchased a new car. Mrs. Craven reminded him that their good friends had only one child, and as for cars, their next-door neighbors still used a car that was older than theirs. Craven had to admit this, but he felt that she didn't care that much since she didn't drive. It was he who watched the others pass him on the highway. What should he do?

The approach of Arthur Adams was thorough and thoughtful. He examined all the practical and mathematical aspects, and after putting all the pros and cons on a piece of paper—and each one had a price tag associated with it—he made his decision. It was a decision based purely on a cost analysis of the situation. In this case, behavior was based on straightforward economic attitudes.

The second man, Barry Bevans, didn't work out any figures at all. He did think about some, namely what his neighbor's income was. His decision was based on a mixture of jealousy, a need to show people he was upwardly mobile in his job, and probably love of a new car. Bevans obviously had a strong need to project an image of wealth and success, whether true or not.

In the case of Cedric Craven, we do not even know what decision he made. All we can see is that there were a number of strains pulling him various ways, like magnetic forces acting on a group of small pieces of iron. He was worried about depreciation on his old car. He was bothered by the slow acceleration of his old car. He saw a neighbor with a new car. All these forces were pushing him to buy. Then he thought of the furniture he needed to purchase, of the recreation room that should be fixed up for his growing children, and so on. These factors were pushing him not to buy, since he wished to spend only so much money at this time. How he decided is left up in the air. The determinants of Craven's behavior are more complex than in the cases of the other two men, whose motives could be guessed at.

Reactions at Work

The situations just discussed involve people responding to needs and pressures basically outside their workplace. There are outside influences on them, reflected by such questions as, "What will the neighbors think?" and "Should I go more into debt in order to buy both car and furniture?" Some of the answers to these questions will depend on an individual's social and moral background. However, since we are considering management situations, let's look also at what will happen to different people in a workplace situation.

Let's take David Donald, a man in his forties, who has been with a firm for many years. He has a secure, even personality. The firm is very conservatively managed, the rules are quite strict, and the managers are considered tough. Mr. Donald has been fairly successful in the firm and is considered to have done many good jobs for the company. On his last assignment, he made a real mistake which caused the firm to lose some potential income. Mr. Donald's manager called him in and spoke to him about the mistake in a tough, serious manner.

Young Everett Ever is employed by this same firm. He joined the company some eight months ago and has been getting along reasonably well for a newcomer. As an individual, he has not had much success in life, although he did quite well in school and in previous jobs. He lost his girl to someone else and does not have much of a secure picture of himself. One day, he makes a real mistake on the job and is sharply criticized by his manager in the usual company manner.

Let's go to another firm, where Frank Factor, who is very much like our Mr. Ever, works. He, too, is fairly young and fairly new on the job. When he makes a sizeable mistake, his manager calls him in, and the conversation goes something like this:

"Frank, since you have come here, you have shown fairly good promise. I was pleased, as I told you, with the way you handled the spring-load set situation. But I am puzzled by what you did with the jig-bearing problem the other day. What do you think?"

"I think I did very poorly, sir."

"Those are the facts, Frank. What I am trying to find out is why. I am sure that you have the ability to handle it, as you have shown several times. Why did it go badly this time?"

"I am trying to think about it and find out the answer."

"Why didn't you come to see me right away?"

"I guess I couldn't, sir. When the first thing happened, I knew I was in trouble but hoped I could save the situation. When it was all done, I was afraid for my job."

"Frank, we do let people go who don't make it here. I don't think you will be one of those. In fact, I'm sure of that. What I would like to do with you now is go over the problem step by step together, to find out what happened and see how we can prevent it from happening again. Do you agree?"

"Yes, sir."

How do you think these three men reacted?

In Mr. Donald's case, he had a pretty positive picture of himself and a good work record with the company. He may have been slightly worried by the failure, but he took it in stride even with the dressing down he received. He may not have had much respect for his manager and the firm for their treatment of him, but passed it off. If another position with another firm had come up, he might have moved for little increase in income, provided, of course, there were no problems with pension rights and other benefits.

In Mr. Ever's case, he did not have much personal strength, much ego, and, of course, much history with the firm. Even if his manager did not fire him—as he might have—he would be a tense, scared worker for some time to come, and though he might do his minimum share for the firm, he would hesitate to do more in case other problems cropped up.

What about Mr. Factor? He obviously would have been worried about his failure, but after his interview with his boss would undoubtedly feel extremely relieved, and his ego strength, which wasn't great to start off with and sagged badly after the event, would probably have gone back up again or even increased from where he started. Other things being equal, Factor would have contributed more to the firm in the future.

These three business situations illustrate the need to know what determines individual behavior when we manage people. While Donald could be treated roughly and this would not affect his behavior, it certainly would affect his loyalty. He might very well leave the firm whenever a good position turned up elsewhere. The manner in which Ever was handled would certainly not improve his performance with the company in the way that Factor's was almost certain to. Factor's treatment would make him a strong member of a loyal group as well as a productive one. And these two results are obviously what good managers should aim to achieve. Understanding why people behave as they do is critical to achieving them.

FACTS AND ASSUMPTIONS ABOUT BEHAVIOR

What we have examined here highlights basic facts of human nature, assumptions made by managers and others about people in general, and the complex of factors which influence our behavior. Let's examine these in order.

What are the basic factors in human behavior as psychologists see them? First, there is a stimulus response set in our behavior. In other words, there is a causal factor in our way of acting. We respond to a stimulus. Second, our behavior is directed toward some goal. This may be the goal of getting food, buying a car, or being held in high esteem by our friends. Third, our behavior is motivated by our needs, or at least what we think of as our needs. We should note here that people talk about our needs, our motives, and our drives. People assign some differences to these words, but they are roughly synonymous.

What are the assumptions we commonly make about people and their behavior? One is that people are economically motivated. They will, in brief, do anything for a buck—well, almost anything. Another is that people are lazy and in order to get them to do work you have to threaten or push them. Another states that people like to get things done and accept responsibility, and therefore that they should be given opportunities and then left alone for a time. The assumptions vary, and some are not realized consciously. They lie deep down within us, and depend on our upbringing, our cultural background, and our experiences.

Somehow we like to believe that all people underneath are the same and, therefore, that they are all pretty much like ourselves (although we might exclude ourselves, since many of us think we are rather exceptional). Up to a point people are the same: they get hungry, they bleed when hurt, and so on. But different times and different cultures make people different.

Social anthropologist and author Edward Hall tells many interesting stories of this in his books. One of the most interesting ones in his latest volume *Beyond Culture** describes a visit to Japan. On this particular visit, Hall was lodged in a hotel in downtown Tokyo which had both European- and Japanese-style rooms. On the eleventh day of his stay there he came back one afternoon and picked up his key. As soon as he entered his room, he realized that he was in the wrong room. He was extremely upset and checked his key again. It was his room number, but the belongings there were not his. He dashed back to the lobby. What had happened? He had liked the room; was he being told to get out for something he had done?

Indeed, he had been moved because the room he was in had been reserved in advance by someone else, and the hotel had made the change. He was very annoyed but obtained the key to his new room. There he found that everything was where he had left it in the old room. This had never happened to him at an American hotel in Japan. The Japanese must think that he was a very low status person who could be shoved around from room to room and he could take it or leave it.

The actual explanation was quite different. He was considered a friend, and when the hotel had to honor the advance reservation for his room, management quietly moved all his belongings to another room, even placed them in equivalent positions in the new room. If the hotel people hadn't thought of him as a friend staying in their home, they would not have done what they did. Thus

*New York: Doubleday, 1976.

Hall's American-style version of what had happened was completely wrong.

This is only one example among thousands illustrating different cultural attitudes. When a manager deals with people of different backgrounds, he has to take these differences into account. Especially in a multicultural country, these differences can be extreme and certainly very important to the individuals involved. In short, a manager must be prepared for people interpreting his or other people's actions in unexpected ways.

An acquaintance of mine who years ago studied attitudes at meetings and conferences of the United Nations told me a story of an Arab holding conversation with an Englishman at a cocktail party given by some agency of the United Nations. These men were talking together in a large room. Culturally, most Westerners like to keep a few feet apart during polite conversation; they only get close for very intimate talk. These distances are, however, not universally accepted. Many Middle East people hold polite conversation almost eyeball-to-eyeball. At the reception, the Englishman kept moving backward in order to maintain his conversational distance. The Arab kept moving forward to maintain his conversational distance. Thus the duo waltzed around the room during their talk. These little differences depend on our cultural background and upbringing, and most of us probably do not even think about them. They are some of the little things which make us different. And there are many more.

Putting all this together, we can say that our performance on the job depends on ourselves and the many facets that make up our individuality, including our goals and needs, and also on the environment in which we work. In this environment we must include the assumptions made about people by our bosses, as well as the political, social, and cultural environment in which we live.

We act to do something. If we have no goals, then we are merely drifting. And even the drifter probably has a goal, if it is only to remove himself from active society.

Let's look at the whole environment to understand the impact it has. In Figure 1, the inner boundary is our immediate organization, its policies, procedures, and attitudes to its workers. The next

Figure I. Factors affecting our work behavior.

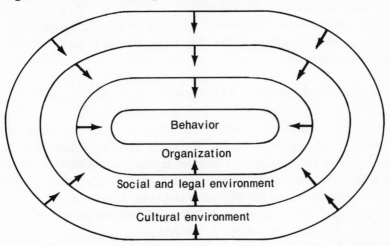

boundary is the legal and social one—basically our country but also including state, municipal, and other laws. The final boundary is the culturally determined one, which we are often unaware of. As someone remarked about this environment: fish are not aware that they are swimming in water! (This remark was obviously made before our days of advanced pollution.)

Dealing with people in the workplace is not simple. In the past very few managers felt it necessary to have this kind of knowledge: it wasn't considered as important as knowing how the machinery operated. This attitude has changed recently, but knowledge of how to deal with people is still not widespread enough in practice. Basically we run into problems because we have no overall knowledge of why people behave as they do. We tend to look for confirmation of our own ideas and do no real testing of assumptions that we may have, such as that people only do things for money or that most people are lazy and require a good kick to get them going. Information that might contradict our own ideas is generally unconsciously blocked out. Our own ideas are culturally determined and most of us appear to be unaware that individuals of other cultural backgrounds may not react to events in the same way that we do.

Other things can lead to problems with people as well. Lack of clear-cut policies and procedures in the organization is one of these. Inability to communicate properly is another major factor. This problem is a big one and will be dealt with more extensively in a later chapter.

Impossible Task for a Manager?

From what we have written, it might seem that every manager should have a year or two of full-time study to acquire a good knowledge of why people behave as they do. Otherwise how would it be possible to obtain this knowledge and still have time left over to carry out the necessary tasks associated with every job? If this were true, managers might be so bogged down that they wouldn't be able to do their jobs properly.

Fortunately a manager does not have to become a psychologist and sociologist and have some other expertise as well. Even with all their knowledge, very few well-trained experts in human behavior could run an organization successfully. What managers require are some of the fundamentals of these sciences, and acquiring this knowledge does not take years. A high literacy in the fields is not required. What is essential is an understanding of the operational knowledge and some practice in applying it.

Questions for Review

(Use extra sheets of paper where required.)

1. List some of the difficulties encountered in managing people.

_____

_____

_____

_____

_____

_____

2. Choose two people in your workplace (or whom you know), one who is similar to you in thinking and feeling, and another who

is not similar to you in a number of major areas in thinking and feeling. Then explain what you think the similarities and dissimilarities are.

Similar person: _____

_____

_____

_____

_____

Dissimilar person: _____

_____

_____

_____

_____

3. Give some examples of how the different cultural backgrounds and upbringing of people determine the way they act.

_____

_____

_____

4. Rate two managers you know on the clarity of their intentions when dealing with subordinates and their ability to communicate.

_____

_____

_____

_____

5. What do you believe are some of the most important things a manager should be aware of?

_____

_____

_____

_____

_____

THE NEEDS AND WANTS OF PEOPLE

As we have already pointed out, years ago it was believed that man was an "economic and rational" being. He did things for financial gain and within the limits of his knowledge, in an orderly fashion. Somehow people have always wished to put order into everything, including human behavior. Not to do so was equated with sin. Many people have preached about the order in nature and how we should strive to follow the natural pattern. Anyone who has tried to grow a garden knows that there is little mechanical order in nature. There are overall orderly concepts, the laws, so-called, of nature. In practice there tends to be limited chaos. Those who deal with the practical side of nature and not the textbook side realize this. Practical management fits into this same category: it cannot be mechanized.

Much of the mechanical thinking about workers and management is said to come from Frederick Winslow Taylor, the American engineer who pioneered time and motion study. In this mechanistic tradition, jobs are examined mechanically and specific methods to do specific jobs taught to selected workers in order to improve production. In the years before 1900, and for some decades later, much of this activity proved to be worthwhile. Taylor and others are now maligned as having a strictly mechanical approach to the use of people. But those who criticize Taylor forget the times in which he lived, as well as some parts of his writings.

In Taylor's day, most factories were extremely disorganized places with little real planning taking place. There did exist a mixture of short-term planning and doing, but it was generally uncoordinated. Taylor's main contribution was to separate planning from doing. Managers did the planning; workers did the assigned tasks. This was a revolutionary concept, and its acceptance gave a major spurt to the American industrial ascendancy in the world. It had the same multiplying effect on output as systematic agriculture had on the ad hoc method of food growing in primitive societies.

Naturally, it led to the idea that all you needed to do to improve production was to take a rational approach to organizational activities and man as a rational and economic being (the first

Taylor-picked workers made a lot more money than the average worker) and you were well away. The race was on. It led to much reorganization of industry in many countries. Without it, we would be in a considerably less advanced industrial state today.

However, it was only stage one in a natural movement to build a better industrial society. Few recognized the limitations in the early days—it appeared to be the golden answer to many people, bosses and workers alike, when it came to production problems. It was the panacea. But while it boosted industries to much higher production levels, it began to show its flaws. It didn't always work as planned—far from it at times.

Things began to turn up in the literature—they showed up in actuality many times and many years before but were not recorded—that indicated that somehow rational and economic man was doing some crazy things. There were times when conditions of production were such that followers of Taylor would have forecast decreases; other times when increases might have been forecast.

What was happening?

The Work of Elton Mayo

Times were changing, and people were possibly reacting to the changing environment, at least in the more advanced industrial countries. In the early 1920s a University of Pennsylvania professor named Elton Mayo noted the emerging of an informal type of worker grouping in a textile mill. Later, when he had moved on to Harvard, he did his famous work at the Hawthorne plant of the Western Electric Company in Chicago.

The Hawthorne research extends over the period from 1927 to 1932. Taylor-style engineers were working on illumination problems and efficiency. But the production rates of the workers didn't respond as they were supposed to. Basically, during the experiment workers were increasing production even when light was reduced almost to moonlight strength. Mayo came in and worked with the employees in setting length of workday, rest periods, and so on. On the basis of his previous experience, he felt that the workers were grouping together because of a basic need for cooperation—something companies completely neglected, as workers were treated for the most part as replaceable units. What increased production, even with poorer lighting, was the cooperative spirit among the workers and the feeling that they were being treated as important—a spinoff from the experiment.

To test his thinking, Mayo organized 20,000 interviews in an attempt to see what was on the minds of the people working in a plant. The result was a confirmation of the importance of the human spirit among the employees in an enterprise and their working together to facilitate production (or, if they wished to, to hinder productivity).

This was the start of study in behavioral sciences, an investigation of the human factors influencing the work activities in any organization. It drew from clinical psychology, anthropology, sociology, and other disciplines and tried to set up a factual research base for the studies.

A very strong example of the social group force in industry and its effect on productivity was illustrated in Britain after World War II. A new mining technology was being introduced for the coal mines.* Originally, mining was carried on with small groups of men working closely together. In each group, one or two of the workers would be skilled in getting the coal free from the veins while the others loaded it in small wagons and transported it. A great comradeship arose between the men in each group; men were selected by the leader of the group and worked in their own mine area. This comradeship was undoubtedly heightened by the danger involved in the work and the need for members of each group to get along well together and look out for the others.

The location of the coal seams in the country and technological advances led to the introduction of a new technique aimed at increasing production. The changes called for teams of some 40 to 50 men working together, and members of the team were often working alone in small tunnels, with the group spread out over a hundred yards and often more. The actual production results with

*Reported by E. L. Trist and E. K. Bamforth in *Human Relations* (1951), 4:3–38.

the advanced machinery were lower than those achieved by the old methods. The teams had been broken up, the comradeship of the small group working together destroyed, being replaced by individuals working by themselves out of easy reach of mates. The dangers of the job focused on the lone individual, who was no longer protected by group trust and spirit.

The mechanistic approach to the employee exemplifies a central assumption owners and managers made about people in the workplace. It has its roots in the slavery and serfdom of previous centuries, as well as the developing production techniques of modern societies. Though man was known to have sexual and other social attitudes away from the workplace, at work he was a mechanical thing, another piece of the machinery rolling out products. When a man didn't fit into this setup, he was called lazy, shiftless, and the like. Reactions to this type of treatment were controlled in earlier days due to the fear of losing jobs. Later on, when workers became more aggressive and demanded more humane approaches, there were demonstrations, strikes, and the formation of trade unions. Few and far apart were people like Robert Owen, the early nineteenth-century British industrialist and reformer who had positive and human assumptions about his workers.

McGregor and Management Assumptions about People

The psychologist Douglas McGregor—we should call him a behavioral scientist—examined the assumptions normally made about people at work in organizations.* He felt that the basic assumptions of owners and managers greatly affected the way they went about their management tasks as well as the way organizational structures were built and run. On one side he placed the following assumptions:

- The average individual inherently dislikes work and tends to avoid it if he can.

*The Human Side of Enterprise (New York: McGraw-Hill Book Company, 1960).

- Most individuals have to be pushed, directed, controlled, and threatened with dire consequences in order to get them to do enough to carry on with the work of an organization.
- Most people prefer to be directed, because they have little ambition, no desire for responsibility, and are anxious about security above all.

On the other side McGregor placed these assumptions:

- People do physical work or mental work as naturally as they do play or rest.
- People will show self-discipline and direction when they are committed to the objectives of an activity.
- Commitment to the objectives is related to the rewards associated with their achievement.
- The average person in a proper setting not only learns to accept responsibility but also seeks it out.
- The capacity to contribute imaginatively and creatively to the solving of the problems of an organization is widely distributed among people, not narrowly.

Now it is easy to suppose that if any manager looked inside himself and recognized the various combinations of assumptions, he could better understand how he acted in practice. He might also conclude that his assumptions about people varied at times with what was happening, the mix of people working for him, the tasks to be performed, and so on. Thus he may act differently depending upon circumstances. Understanding these assumptions, he felt, could make better managers out of each one.

Unfortunately, the first set of assumptions, known as Theory X, was associated with the "bad" guys. The second set is known as Theory Y and is associated with the "good" guys. McGregor felt that Theory Y represented a truer set of assumptions about people and hoped that they would become part of management thinking one day. His main emphasis in presenting them, however, was on getting managers to examine their assumptions about people.

Basic Needs

Other scientists were researching the wants, needs, motives, or drives that move or help people move to do things. What goes into making a human being, aside from the physical aspects and the clinical subconscious items examined by Freud and others practicing psychiatry? Are there building blocks or motives or drives or needs or what have you? Is there something analogous to a skeletal structure, a musculature structure, a blood circulation system, and so on in the nonphysical side of man? How are we composed in this respect? Are there common structures?

If there are, then knowledge of them would be vitally important to any manager. He would know something about people, and this knowledge could help him reduce the puzzling complexity of human behavior to certain basic qualities, some of them emotional, some logical. In today's world, the only real way to change people is to get them to change themselves. Aside from body, then, what are we all about?

The psychologist Abraham Maslow, in considering the basic needs of man and the interrelationships between these needs, came to the conclusion that there were five basic drives. The primary needs of all people are physiological ones, that is, the need for food, drink, clothes, shelter, and the like. When these needs are unfulfilled, the drive to satisfy them can build up enormous pressures and involve great personal risk-taking. Many people in this world live at a low level of satisfaction of these primary needs all their lives. They will fight animals in forests for food or one another in cities for food and drink. For most people who do not achieve some satisfaction regularly of their physiological needs, all other needs are unimportant. The need also comes in surges; once satisfied, it is dormant for a time. Then it starts up again and hopefully becomes satisfied again and so is quiet once more. And on and on.

The next need is one for safety and security. We need a place to be where we can live and work in safety and security. Though this need may assume an important role a few times, it does not have the endless repetitive pattern of the first need. In most Western countries, we do achieve a fair amount of safety and security, although the crime rate in many cities does again trigger this need. However, a person will give up safety and security if he is hungry—that is, a hungry person will take many chances to obtain food—and the same thing holds for other physiological needs.

Having satisfied the first two basic needs, people's next requirement involves belonging, being part of a group, being accepted as a member of a clan, a family, an association, or the like. We need this sense of belonging, and most Western people get some amount of this in families, churches, sometimes even in workplaces. Again, this need will fade in importance if safety and security needs or physiological ones become pronounced.

The fourth need is for a sense of esteem and status. This means not only acceptance by friends and neighbors but being looked up to for various reasons. Some satisfy this need with big houses and big cars or both, some with growing the best roses in the neighborhood, others with thoughtful social service activities in hospitals or elsewhere. For many people, this need is felt to be satisfied if others in the workplace regularly turn to them and ask for their opinion on various matters. There are many ways to obtain esteem and status, and once the first three needs are pretty well satisfied, we want to satisfy this fourth need. When satisfied, it too may lie quiescent within us for some time.

The fifth and final need is somewhat different and is often not satisfied in most of us. It is the need to achieve self-fulfillment, to lead a creative, interesting life, one that utilizes our knowledge and abilities in a creative fashion. We want to make the fullest use of our potential. This need is rarely tapped if the other four are generally not fulfilled, and, unlike them, it doesn't seem to die down for a time but requires continuous feeding.

Maslow's hierarchy of needs, as the five are called, is often illustrated in the form of a pyramid, with the physiological needs forming the base and the self-fulfillment need forming the top of the pyramid. The idea is to show that the bottom need is supposed to be satisfied before the next one becomes important to a person, and so on up the layers of the pyramid. There is some controversy as to whether this is true, but for our purposes the argument is not terribly important. The point is that the needs and their order of appearance, perfect or not, give us some basic understanding of people in general. They provide the underpinnings for our understanding of why we behave as we do. However, there are many steps beyond this before we can appreciate how managers can deal positively and effectively with people.

INDIVIDUAL MOTIVES

The psychologist David McClelland was interested in individual differences between people's drives or needs. He wanted to examine the forces that made one individual strive more to feed himself when hungry than another, for example. Although he essentially agreed with the basic needs as catalogued by Maslow, he wanted to know what determines the individual strength of the drive to security or self-esteem or self-fulfillment. What he and others arrived at are the *individual motives* that turn on our engines to satisfy our individual needs. We use the term motives here to differentiate them somewhat from what Maslow called needs. The two ideas are not in contradiction with each other; rather, McClelland provides an extension of Maslow's thinking in that he pinpoints individual drives rather than general mass drives.

Three motives emerged from McClelland's research work: the need for achievement, the need for affiliation, and the need for power. To simplify things, we shall refer to them as achievement, affiliation, and power. The researchers found ways to measure these three motives which are distributed in us in various proportions, with one of the three possibly dominating the others. They appear to be bred in us by our experiences, including our education and training. Therefore, they can be altered somewhat by further training and experiences.

Achievement measures the desire to get things done for the sake of doing them and a willingness to take chances in accomplishing tasks when the odds are pretty good. This person is no gambler; he wants to see the possibilities and measure his capabilities of accomplishment before exerting himself. He will stretch himself to accomplish possible objectives and, therefore, have a feeling of personal achievement. If he gambles and wins, there is no sense of personal achievement. His rewards have little meaning except that they demonstrate successful accomplishment. They are necessary for that reason and because the individual needs constant feedback on how he is doing. When an individual with a strong push to achieve starts a job, he will generally remain with it until it is completed. However, as indicated, he does need to know regularly how things are going; he can't operate in the dark for long. He prefers a challenge with a time factor built in, but not a Herculean task which may be near-impossible to accomplish. He also enjoys the responsibility of a challenging task and sets up pretty high standards for himself in meeting the challenge. People with a high amount of achievement concern in their makeup include our entrepreneurs, salespeople (at least the better ones), doctors, and middle managers.

Great strength showing up in affiliation demonstrates an interest in working closely with people in groups, a concern for sympathetic comradeship. In sports you can often tell these people because they prefer team games to one-to-one games, which are favored by the achievement types. Affiliation-oriented people go out of their way to make friends, especially when new people are in a group to which they belong. They are also concerned with having a friendly relationship with their bosses and may go to great lengths to win friendship. Generally, counselors belong to this group, as do nurses and, to a certain extent, teachers.

People with strong power concerns like to be in control of people. They enjoy good arguments, especially when they emerge on top. They also like to give orders to others and enjoy the trappings of power, such as impressive titles, fancy offices, and prestige connections. They will often be so strongly motivated this way that they will not consult others when they need help. People in this area category often are politicians, senior managers, or teachers. Understanding the motives and their strengths in individual people can be extremely useful in the selection process as well as in providing the proper climate for people to operate successfully.

Questions for Review

(Use extra paper where required.)

1. Explain the ideas which Elton Mayo uncovered at Hawthorne. Give examples which demonstrate his ideas from what you have read and heard and from your own experiences.

_____

_____

_____

_____

2. What are the basic assumptions which McGregor stated are held by managers about people? Classify them under X and Y assumptions.

_____

_____

_____

_____

3. Which of the above items do you fully agree with? Which do you strongly disagree with?

_____

_____

_____

4. List the basic needs of people, according to Maslow, and give examples for each need.

_____

_____

_____

_____

5. Do you think that these needs are complete and in order? Explain why.

_____

_____

_____

6. What are the main individual motives explored by McClelland? How do they demonstrate their existence in individuals?

_____

_____

_____

_____

7. Which of the following pastimes are likely to be engaged in by a person with a high achievement need, and which are likely to appeal to a person with a high affiliation need? (Use _A_ for achievement and _F_ for affiliation.)

Chess_____ Skiing_____ Fencing_____ Bridge_____
Squash_____ Swimming_____ Tennis_____ Skating_____ Ping Pong_____ Baseball_____ Football_____

Explain your reasoning in at least two cases in each area.

_____

_____

_____

_____

8. Consider the following descriptions of people, and check in the appropriate column what you feel may be their strongest motive (McClelland style).

PERCEPTION

Before going more fully into the area of motivation, we will look at the problem of perception. What we call our reality is how we perceive things, whether this corresponds to external reality or not. Some philosophers will argue that there is actually no external reality, for everything is perceived through our senses and interpreted through our experiences. We will not go into this argument here. Our basic point relates to Robert Burns's famous line: "To see ourselves as others see us."

If we are dealing with a person as a manager does with an individual working for him (or even vice versa), it is not good enough to proceed on our perception of this person, unless his own

	Orientation		
	Achievement	*Affiliation*	*Power*
1. He is eager to accept responsibility and sets high standards for himself.			
2. He enjoys telling other people how to do things.			
3. He is always interested in finding out how he is doing.			
4. He gets a kick out of a good argument.			
5. He generally finishes any task he sets out to do.			
6. He goes out of his way to make friends, especially newcomers to a group he is in.			
7. Status symbols are very important to him and he frequently talks about them in conversations or discussions.			
8. He is almost always trying to make out with managers above him.			

perception of himself is pretty similar. For an individual's reality is his self-perception, and if we want to be successful in dealing with people, we must start from how they see themselves. There can be no other starting point.

Henry Ford once remarked, "Whether you think you can or you think you can't, you are right." Testing the validity of the relationship between perception and reality is generally quite easy. Speak to a few acquaintances, at work or in other organizations, and use this little test. This may work with close friends, but not as well. It is best to do the experiment with acquaintances. Make up a few statements along these lines*:

If a person works hard, he's sure to head for the top.
I like my own appearance.
Our president will be feted in the future.
The press loves to highlight violence.
School principals should punish children with the strap.
I am very hesitant in expressing my admiration for others.
I always vote in all elections.
Trade unions have far too much power.

Prepare a dozen or so comments of this type. Then on a zero to 10 scale, guess how you think each acquaintance would rate himself on each item. If you think, for example, that he really does not like his appearance, give him a zero; if you believe that he is very proud of his appearance, give him a 10; if you think he has no opinion one way or the other, give him a 5, which is the midpoint. And do the same for all the items. At the same time request each individual to rate himself on all the items.

After the ratings are completed, compare your ratings of each individual with their own. You will discover to your surprise that many of the scores are far apart. You will probably also notice differences when doing this exercise with close friends. If any manager would perform this test with his subordinates, using basically more job-related criteria, the differences in perception would probably surprise him, too.

Self-Perception

A critical aspect of how we are motivated and react to people and other stimuli is how we see ourselves. Undoubtedly a number of

*Adapted from the *1976 Annual Handbook for Group Facilitators,* edited by L. W. Pfeiffer and L. E. Jones. La Jolla, Calif.: University Associates, Inc.

things go into forming our self-concept, including our childhood and how our parents dealt with us, the rules learned from success or failure in playing with peers, the record of the gains and losses in our lives, our notion of what rewards we are seeking and deserve, and our innate need for achievement.

Perception, and particularly self-perception, is not easy to understand. We are all aware that we may not see others the same way they see themselves. We all have blind spots that hide some of our strengths and weaknesses from ourselves. Each one of us operates from his or her own perceptions, including the blind spots. However, to successfully relate to people and in particular to manage them, we have to start with how they perceive themselves, realizing that this is only part of the full picture and that we ourselves do not have the really true view.

What Our Senses Do

We have examined broadly how our perception of others (and ourselves) can lead to relationships that get off on the wrong foot. If you think that the example taken—where we compared our perception of people along certain lines with their own—involves a lot more than mistaken stimuli, just consider a few simpler illustrations.

Many people believe that there are such things as moving pictures. When they go to a movie house they generally see events taking place as if they were viewing them in some house or on some streets. (We will, of course, have to omit bizarre films for this purpose.) People are moving, cars are moving, and so on. However, if you examine the reel of film, you know that it consists only of still pictures. Each picture is just slightly different from the previous one. As the reel moves through the projector, a shutter movement shows us one still picture quickly following another. Our eyes do not detect this, for the speed with which it is done is too fast for us. What we see is a picture, then quickly a next one almost the same, and quickly another, and so on. The eyes and the brain cannot adjust to the speed, and so we see people and objects "moving." The reality is actually different, as we have just described.

Chairs in a Hallway

Take a look now at the drawing in Figure 2. It looks like a corridor in a strange movie. Can you estimate the size of the chair in the foreground relative to that of the chair in the background of the picture? Just make a rough guess. Then take a ruler and measure the actual size of each chair. Better still, draw a duplicate of the chair in the distance and place it beside the chair in the front. (All chairs are the same size.)

Figure 2. Test your perception: Which chair is the biggest?

These examples of moving pictures and chairs in a hallway illustrate simple optical illusions. The point they make is that if our brains react in this manner to relatively straightforward phenomena, how would they react to our attempts to "see" people as they see themselves. We can too easily fool ourselves into believing that our own perception of such a complicated creation as another person is the same as their perception of themselves. Some people claim that you can learn to read people like a book. All I can reply to that is that many people who read the same book will describe it in quite different ways if you ask them to talk about it.

The important thing for a manager to remember is not how to try and become a people expert, but that these differences in perception do exist. Remembering this when you deal with people will help you adjust your methods of doing so, as you see what responses you generate. It should also make you more conscious of how people perceive you. This can prevent many a "don't be so stupid" or "I've made it completely clear" statement.

People tend to see things depending on their own needs. We try to ignore or bury unpleasant items or those we fear. This is healthy in part, since it tends to make us generally concentrate on more positive aspects of ourselves. However, it could be self-deceptive, for buried items may come in force to disturb us later on. Being conscious of how others see us, we also try to put on some type of act. Unfortunately or not, we can generally see through others' attempts to present an untrue or distorted view of themselves better than we can see through our own game playing.

Summing Up Perception

To pin some of these ideas down, it is worthwhile repeating some of the information in a different form. What are the steps in becoming aware of things and responding to them? The first stage is receiving data through one of our senses—auditory, visual, or otherwise. Once received, the information is interpreted. In the case of bland or spicy food this may be relatively simple, but even here a judgment of bland or spicy depends on what we have experienced before and are used to. What is spicy to someone is only so-so to another person. In a more complex situation, how we interpret the sense data received depends on many elements in our long or recent history. It could go back to childhood experiences; it could go back to just a short time ago when new data tell us that things are not nearly as bad (or much better) than they appeared to be when previous data were interpreted.

The interpretation of the data leads to a response. If emotion is involved, this may even color our interpretation of the information received: we may wish to shut out some of it. Our response will depend on what we expect to get out of the situation. Our expectancies are involved. If a salesman, for example, is doing relatively poorly and is told by his manager that if he does exactly what the manager says he will triple his commission earnings in short order, the reaction is likely to be negative, for the salesman will not believe it. If the manager told him that if he works with him to do certain things he could increase his take by 30 percent or more, then the salesperson would be more likely to believe it and respond positively.

The final step is the actual response, and this could even be doing nothing.

If a manager wishes to work positively with people, then he has to have some understanding of the basic process of perception as well as an understanding of the basic needs of people and of individual differences. If he treats people as all alike under the skin, he may well accomplish nothing. A manager should break away from stereotypes such as the Theory X assumption that all people are inherently lazy or from more specific prejudices such as that black people are lazier than white people or that Eastern people are not to be trusted. He should also not project his own thinking about himself on others, which is extremely easy for all of us to do.

A useful idea is for a manager to know himself well, because then he can know others more accurately. If he is personally insecure, then he will have problems and mistrust relationships with people. While if he is personally quite secure, he can easily develop warm relationships, for he is not pitting himself against all others and can afford to recognize the good qualities of others. It is something each manager has to work at, and the work is never over.

MOTIVATION

Let us return to the idea that a person's performance is a combination of the relationships between the various aspects of the individual and the climate or environment in which he performs. The question arises of how do you motivate people to perform better?

McGregor said that you don't motivate people. "Man is by nature motivated. He is an organic system, not a mechanical system."* He might have added that a nonmotivated man is a dead one, or at least a pretty sick one. Creating the proper relationships between the characteristics of the individual and his environment in order to change performance is a matter of releasing energy in some ways rather than others, states McGregor.

Psychologist and author Saul Gellerman writes: "What management needs is not so much a method for motivating people as a way of thinking about it." "To be motivated," Gellerman writes, "is to steer one's actions toward certain goals and to commit a certain part of one's energies to reaching them." † The process varies from person to person, but all require individual goals, not general ones. A secret of success here lies not just in understanding the process and making use of it, but also in only trying to change things that are changeable.

To repeat ourselves, we start with people and how they perceive themselves, and then arrange things in the environment to bring out the most productive aspects of people and also, though probably on a lesser scale, attempt to influence and change the characteristics of the individual. In many cases individual characteristics are influenced more effectively by the environment in which the individual works than by any direct attempts to change

*Douglas McGregor, *The Professional Manager* (New York: McGraw-Hill Book Company, 1967), p. 10.
† Saul W. Gellerman, *Management by Motivation* (New York: American Management Association, 1968), pp. 10, 54.

people so as to make them fit into the environment. Naturally this means careful selection procedures so that a better working relationship can be established. Every individual cannot be hammered into shape to be in tune with the environment, no matter how wonderful it may appear to be. On the other hand, the environment cannot be changed drastically to fit every individual without impairing economic performance. Many times something has to go. Sometimes this may be the worker; sometimes the manager.

The aroused motivation of a person which leads him to take action is said to be a product of three things: the *basic motive*, the person's *expectancy* of reaching the goal, and the perceived *incentive* value of the goal (see Figure 3). The basic motive was probably acquired over the years from childhood on. This would be either achievement, affiliation, or power or some mixture of the three. Expectancy and incentive would depend on the experiences of the person and be greatly influenced by the environment, which in turn is greatly influenced by the manager, directly or indirectly.

J. W. Atkinson had a useful way of showing how the factors we are discussing work in an individual. Here is his view: *

- Normal people have variable sources of potential energy.
- Normal people have basic motives or needs, which we can think of as valves that channel the energy and regulate the flow.
- Strong motives are like valves that open easily and have a larger aperture for energy flow, generally due to frequent use.
- Weak motives are like tight, sticky valves, which, even when open, allow only a limited flow.
- Whether or not the motive leads to action depends on the specific situation in which a person finds himself.
- By changing the nature of the situation, different motives can be aroused or made stronger or weaker.

*Adapted from *An Introduction to Motivation* (New York: Van Nostrand, 1964).

Figure 3. Factors in taking action.

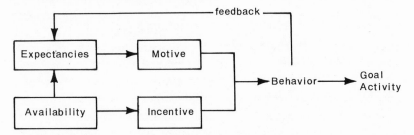

Some research shows that the need for achievement, which is a useful need not only in a manager but in all employees, is aroused by such things as responsibility, support, rewards and punishment, conflict, standards, and risks. A good manager should, therefore, know what are the basic underlying motives in his people and the best ways to arouse them. He should help create the organizational climate that is critical to high performance. We shall be discussing more on this topic in the chapter on organization.

The Work of Herzberg

In a study of the attitudes of people toward their jobs, psychologist Frederick Herzberg and his associates came across a number of interesting facts.* They investigated these more thoroughly, and the information they gathered seems to point to two major factors that influence the motivation of people at work.

The first of these consists of what are called hygienic factors. Nobody is really turned on by them and goes ahead with his work with renewed vigor, but everybody feels dissatisfied if these items are not present. Here they are:

Receiving a salary increase.
Having good relations with supervisors.
Having beneficial personnel policies.

*Frederick Herzberg et al., *The Motivation to Work,* 2nd ed. (New York: John Wiley & Sons, Inc., 1959).

Having a prestige type of job.
Having a competent supervisor.
Having good relationships with subordinates.
Having a secure job.
Meeting financial family needs and expectations.
Liking people you work with.
Good physical and social surroundings.

A look at all these items shows that they are mainly related to the environment in which a job is being performed. The items that compose the second factor are called motivators. They are supposed to be the ones that really move people to do better at their work. They are:

Seeing the results of your work.
Performing creative work.
Receiving more responsibility.
Receiving advancement.
Receiving praise and recognition.
Having the possibility of growth in skill.

These are related to the performance of the work itself. There is an obvious connection between these and Maslow's self-esteem and self-fulfillment needs, which we looked at a while back. The hygenic factors are more related to the lower needs pointed out by Maslow, involving such things as physiological needs and security.

A number of people have argued against the inclusion of "receiving a salary increase" in the hygienic factors rather than the motivators. The fact that once an increase is received, there is a period of contentment followed by a feeling that more money is required appears to support Herzberg. However, others state that to many, a salary increase is not just more money but a measure of success and could be similar to receiving praise and recognition. However, since many salary increases, especially at lower levels, are across the board, this argument would hardly apply.

The Case of the Green and the Yellow Units

Some years ago Dr. Shoukry Saleh, now at the University of Waterloo, and I carried out research incorporating the two Herzberg factors into a study of two major plants owned by the same company. The results are quite interesting, and the story is, I believe, worth spelling out in a little more detail.

The two units were chosen for the study because of the difference in their management style and organizational concepts. They are also, or were at the time of the study, fairly similar in size, each having some 700 members on staff with around 70 members in management. However, there are some significant differences between the two operations. Although both are manufacturing units, the products of the participative-management unit (which we shall refer to as the green unit) are far more esoteric than those of the other plant (the yellow unit). The yellow unit is located in a small town where the population is numbered in thousands, whereas the participative (green) plant is located in a fairly large center with the population numbering hundreds of thousands. The two units of the organization operate under the general philosophy of management of the parent company and are geared to follow the objectives of the organization as a whole.

It should be emphasized here that the company is considered to be highly progressive and deeply concerned with the development of all its people, both technically and from a management point of view. It has a long history of interesting personnel policies and has always participated in development programs, either its own or those offered through outside educational organizations.

The yellow unit was patterned on the fairly traditional hierarchical pattern of management. It appeared to be well managed and a credit to the organization as a whole. The green unit was new and had been conceived as a "man–machine" operation with a systems orientation rather than a departmental structure. It was created to purposefully and consciously build a social and economic environment that would stimulate growth in both individuals and groups. The latest thinking of behavioral scientists was considered in the development of its organizational structure.

Human resources were given equal billing with technical resources. Managers had the job of helping the groups they headed to achieve their goals rather than employing authoritarian methods. Much group problem solving was involved and much time taken in achieving consensus. Time clocks were thrown out, coffee breaks and lunch periods unscheduled.

The organizers of the scheme were aware that the planning stage and the shakedown would last several years. They were confident that when they refined their mode of operation, they would demonstrate commercial and social success. The board of directors of the parent firm sanctioned the new concept. After several years of operations, the green unit was showing, for a time anyway, as high a rate of contributions to profit as any unit in the firm. Employee turnover was below the 2 percent level per month—a low rate for this type of industry—and the unit was scheduled for a great expansion. This does not indicate that other units, such as the yellow one, were not operating well. The company, as a whole, has been very successful.

The green unit, as mentioned, was manufacturing esoteric products in the high-growth, fast-changing electronics area, and engineering changes would reduce costs quite drastically, as labor costs ran at about half as many percentage points of total costs as did those of the yellow unit.

One can readily see many problems in setting up the green unit. It required people to play roles rather than do jobs; it required people to enter into decision making rather than to take orders; it placed people in a fluid, almost unstructured type of operation rather than in a structured one; and it gave people management-type positions without the authority normally associated with them.

A few words should be said about the yellow unit. It manufactured a fairly stable diet of company products in order to maintain employment in the town as well as to give a fair return on investment to the company. It also made some very out-of-the-ordinary products and its history is interesting. The plant was started shortly after World War II and manufactured a wide variety of commercial products ranging from fairly small items for use in the home to rather large electrical engineering items. During the Korean War it moved into defense production and cut back on its commercial production. Movement into the defense fields required bringing in a large staff of engineers and technicians. It was here that the company's now large research and development department was started. The big R&D organization is no longer located with the yellow unit, although a local branch is there.

In the early sixties it was decided that defense requirements were an uncertain quantity and, therefore, that the firm should have a more stable product base. With the company reorganization, the outlook for the yellow unit was for a 90 percent dollar diet of stable equipment and about 10 percent in dollar terms in the more sophisticated manufacturing areas. From the population point of view, fewer than 10 percent would work on the more sophisticated type of equipment.

Without going into details of how the research was carried out, the information obtained revealed the following facts.

Differences in motivation items. First, in regard to the six items mentioned as motivating ones (see Table 1), it should be mentioned that by combining all the items we were able to come up with a general motivating score as well as scores for each separate item. Two of the six items recorded show a great deal of sig-

Table 1. Differences in motivating items between the yellow and the green units.

| | Mean | | Significant |
Item	Yellow	Green	Difference
Seeing results of work	9.583	11.027	
Performing creative work	6.396	9.676	Yes
Receiving more responsibility	7.813	8.811	
Receiving advancement	8.917	9.568	
Receiving praise and recognition	5.708	7.649	Yes
Having possibility of growth in skill	8.854	10.054	
General score	32.271	41.784	Yes

nificant difference. This is particularly true of "performing creative work." The factor called "receiving praise and recognition" is also very significant. Although no other significant differences are shown between the yellow and the green unit, all the motivating factors were higher for the green than for the yellow unit. Though the differences are not significant, they show the overall trend, thus reinforcing the results for the two factors that show pronounced significance. The important general score indicates a great degree of significant difference between the yellow and the green unit. Again, the green score was higher.

Differences in hygienic items. When we scored for the ten hygienic items—and here there was no general score—we came up with the results shown in Table 2. Three items show significant differences: "having beneficial personnel policies," "liking people you work with," and "good physical and social surroundings." Of these, the last shows the most significant difference. Interestingly, for these three items the result pattern is the reverse of that found for the motivators: the higher scores were all shown by the yellow group and not the green group. With respect to the remaining seven factors, it will be noted that the actual scores in five items are higher for the yellow group than for the green group. In one case, "job of special prestige," the figures are extremely close.

In one of the ten items the mean for the green group is higher than that for the yellow group, although the difference is not significant. It is interesting that this factor is "receiving salary increase," an item which can have several connotations in people's minds, such as being a sign of recognition of good work as well as indicating advancement, etc. The overall trend of higher scores for the yellow unit reinforces the significant differences found for three items in this group. This interesting show of differences between two plants operating under the same overall company policies and with capable progressive management reinforces the benefits which managers can obtain by thinking through the two factor items when organizing and directing their operations.

The basic reason for the differences in the two units is the

Table 2. Differences in hygienic items between the yellow and the green units.

Item	Mean Yellow	Green	Significant Difference
Receiving salary increase	7.958	9.081	
Having good relations with supervisor	6.500	5.297	
Having beneficial personnel policies	6.167	4.216	Yes
Job of special prestige	3.021	3.135	
Having a competent supervisor	7.375	7.027	
Having good relationships with subordinates	10.479	10.216	
Having a secure job	6.125	4.243	
Meeting family needs and expectations salarywise	11.167	10.757	
Liking people you work with	8.708	6.486	Yes
Good physical and social surroundings	5.229	2.757	Yes

type of individuals working in them. For example, about half of the employees in the green unit had university degrees and quite a few had more than one degree. Fewer than one in five of those working in the yellow unit had a bachelor's degree. For this reason, the green unit people had less desire to fit into a structured organization than did their fellow employees in the other plant; the nature of the work to be done allowed the green unit to function with less "formal" structure.

It should be noted, however, that when you ranked the scores on all 16 factors, the top five in each plant included three motivators and two hygienic items. Herzberg's ideas appear to fit organizations in general, but people with strong personal drives and commitments require a more intensive climate of motivators than those who are happy to work at more structured and routine tasks. These differences in individuals obviously should be taken into account when setting up organizational units as well as in assigning activities to employees.

Questions for Review

(Use extra paper where required.)

1. Explain point by point the various steps between sensing something and responding to it.

_____

_____

_____

_____

2. Explain a few things about peers or superiors of yours which you feel they are not aware of or were not aware of for some time.

_____

_____

_____

_____

3. Give some perceptions you or a friend had about people or things which you afterward discovered were false. Explain how one of these perceptions was discovered to be false.

_____

_____

_____

_____

4. Explain the difference which Herzberg discovered between motivators and hygiene items. Mention some of the key ones and state what your experience has taught you about them.

_____

_____

_____

_____

Case Study
Roberts Company, Inc.

Read through the following case in the same manner as you did with the case given in Chapter 1. Use the questions at the end as guides and add others if you think they do not cover the situation fully enough. Write down your answers.

The Roberts Company is in the business of supplying parts and services to a broad range of plants. Its services are generally in connection with its parts. It also does some assembly of some of its parts, making a few items and putting them together with parts it purchases from other companies. The firm was founded by John Roberts some 25 years ago and became a fairly successful small firm. It had about 60 employees in all and did a few million dollars' worth of business each year. John Roberts was the firm's chairman of the board as well as president. He was generally the main person to bring in new ideas. The general manager was Paul Sauve, whom Roberts had brought into the firm some eight years previously.

One day Roberts brought in a new item which he felt should be utilized by his firm. A few additions to it would make it a very good seller, he felt. Paul Sauve agreed with Roberts. They discussed the idea with the other members of the board and decided to go ahead. Going ahead meant creating a new department in the firm and getting somebody to do the job. Roberts told Sauve to set up the department and find someone. As the firm believed in hiring from within, if possible, Sauve looked over the list of possible internal candidates. Here is what he found.

Tom Swift—a man in his mid-forties who had been with the firm for some ten years and was now assistant to the head of the parts department, a very important unit of the company. He was not an aggressive person and kept much to himself. He was considered to be doing a relatively good job in his present position. The firm was aware that Swift was doing some soul searching about himself, wondering if he were doomed to stay at his present level for the rest of his life. The head of the parts department was a few years younger than Swift.

Roger Barth—a man in his late twenties, bright and with a better education than Swift. He had been with the firm for a few years and had experience both in sales and inside work. He was well liked around the plant and many looked on him as a comer. He obviously had good potential, but there was no guarantee that he would do a top job. Some of the people around had wondered when Barth would leave if he did not see a future for himself in the plant.

Ross Brown—a year or two younger than Barth, he had also been with the firm a few years but always on outside sales work. Though doing relatively well, he was not the best the company had. He was getting along quite well with most people but tended to be somewhat stand-offish. His uncle was a member of the board of the firm with a substantial financial interest but had never indicated to anyone that his nephew should be given the nod. Sauve would consider Brown a second choice for the position, although an adequate one. However, he did wonder if choosing Brown might ensure that he become president when Roberts stepped down in the coming year, as he had said he would do. Nobody had ever told Sauve that he was slated to succeed Roberts in the senior operating position.

Questions

1. Which of the three should be selected, or should Sauve go outside?
2. What will be the effect on the motivation of the others when one of them—or an outsider—is selected?
3. How should Sauve handle the motivational problems (including his own)?

TRANSACTIONAL ANALYSIS

There is another body of knowledge about people and how they interact which can be very helpful to managers in understanding first, themselves, and second, the people with whom they deal. It can facilitate better communications between people. It is known by the name of transactional analysis, or TA.

In his book *Games People Play*, Canadian psychiatrist Eric Berne, the founder of TA, wrote:

The unit of social intercourse is called a transaction. If two or more people encounter each other in a social aggregation, sooner or later one of them will speak, or give some other indication of acknowledging the presence of the others. This is called a transactional stimulus. Another person will then say or do something which is in some way related to the stimulus, and that is called the transactional response.*

The analysis of these transactions leads to an investigation of what started the stimulus and what brought on the response.

Berne's work was based on the research of another Canadian, the famous neurosurgeon Wilder Penfield. To understand Penfield's work, it is necessary to appreciate a basic problem of brain surgery: in operating on people's brains you can't use an overall anesthetic, because when you probe in the brain, you have to watch for physical reactions and there would be none. So you only use what is needed to kill the pain. While probing with a small electrode in people's brains, Penfield obtained some fascinating reactions. When the electric probe was on a certain spot, patients mentioned a specific moment in their lives. It was both factual and emotional. It was as if that person were actually reliving that specific moment—music, smells, talk, anger, all were recalled. At another spot, another specific incident was recalled. No generalizations, no summaries, and not only facts, but feelings, too. The brain thus appears to be a strange vast computer that records all our individual experiences.

Eric Berne, knowing of Penfield's work, conceived the idea that these "recordings" of experiences and our feelings about the experiences were like tape recordings in our brain. He then postulated the idea that our personality is composed of three key parts, each of which is based on information stored in the brain. He called the parts the Parent, the Adult, and the Child.

The Ego States

Ego States, as Berne named the three parts, are generalizations of the three kinds of stored material. They exist as psychological

*New York: Grove Press, 1964, p. 29.

realities and differ for each one of us, depending on the content of the brain-stored material. Unlike ordinary tape recordings, they cannot be erased and they appear to be replayed often.

The Parent. This state consists of the sum of recordings of unquestioned and imposed experiences as perceived by a person in the first five years of life. They are generally obtained from the pronouncements and examples of parents or parent substitutes and are "unedited."

The Child. This state consists of recordings made at the same time as those of the Parent, but reflect the responses of the child to what he sees and hears. They do not represent the actual truth, just the reaction to what the child sees, hears, and experiences. They are internal in contrast to the Parent ones. The Child records the feelings of discovery and adventure experienced by a child, but tends to be dominated by a sense of inadequacy—that is, the Child feels that he is not as good as he should be, because he is generally being instructed how to behave. For example, the infant who is vigorously told not to go near a hot stove has no ability to reason why not, just a recording that he has to be ordered to do things. This generates a general childhood feeling of self-doubt. Five years of age appears to be the changing age, not because recordings cease to be made but because they generally tend to repeat what has happened previously and because a maturing process is taking place, leading to the development of the Adult.

The Adult. This starts with the youngster beginning to explore and react to his surroundings by himself. It generally begins when the child first crawls about and investigates things. If the Parent is a child's concept of life as *taught* by his parents and the Child is his *felt* concept of life, then the Adult could be referred to as the *thought* concept of life, based on the child's own gathering and processing of data and his own testing of things and events, including the taught ideas coming from parents.

All three ego states can coexist in a person, and any one of them may become dominant at a given time.

How can we use this information? We are always getting stimuli and responses in our jobs. A pair of these Berne called a transaction. If we can understand transactions better, then we can improve them and get better responses to our stimuli in the future. By realizing that transactions between people show us as Child, Adult, or Parent, we can then obtain a better understanding of how to improve the stimulus-response business that is part of our daily lives.

Communication Examples

The following diagrams and examples will help us understand how to make use of some of the elementary ideas in transactional analysis. In the diagrams, P stands for Parent, A for Adult, and C for Child—the three ego states of people. Transactions between two people can be represented by lines going back and forth between the two rows of letters. For the two Adult ego states we would have:

P   P
A ⇄ A
C   C

For a Parent-to-Child relation and a response of Child to Parent we would have:

If, however, the response in this last case was again a Parent-to-Child one, we would get:

This type of crossed-lines response indicates trouble. Communication becomes blocked. Understanding this fact and the basic meaning of the ego states can help us relate to people.

By looking at the crossing of lines in communication, we can see that an Adult-to-Adult response is not always the best way of responding. If someone deals with us as a Parent to a Child, then replying as an Adult to an Adult we get:

A Child-Parent response would not cross lines but may lead nowhere. An Adult-Parent reply might be the best way to start, followed by a move to the Adult-Adult mode. If a stimulus were Child-Parent, an Adult-Adult response would not achieve understanding, maybe not even over time. A Parent-Child response would probably be called for, with a possible move to a more Adult type of discussion:

The actual situation would determine whether it was even necessary to move on to an Adult-Adult transaction. The basic thing to remember is which ego state started the transaction and how to reply without crossing lines in doing so. This works whether one is on the receiving end or sending end. A response to an A to A stimulus that one might initiate might result in a cross, depending on the response. However, if we are aware of this, we can avoid the blockage by first realizing what is happening and not getting aroused and cutting off further discussion but trying to get the transactions on to a basis where further communication can take place profitably.

We have only touched on the subject here, but that is all we need to know in order to help a person perform better as a manager in the human interrelationships which are so essential. Now let us examine some actual transactions.

Practical Examples

Suppose you are a manager in a work situation and you have just explained something to a person working for you. Instead of acknowledging the information, his reply is: "Do you expect me to believe all that? Sounds like everybody else talking around here." If you were to reply, "Cool it. Who do you think you are talking to?" what ego state would you think you were showing? And what do you expect would be the result of that transaction? If you replied that your ego state was that of a Parent, you would be right. And the result would be a flare-up between the two of you.

Now, you may be thoroughly annoyed with your worker over time and are just about ready to fire him, if you can, so maybe you do not worry about how you reply. But that is an exception. Suppose you replied something like this: "That is a pretty strong statement to make. I think we should have a real good rap session with no holds barred." The first response—"Cool it"—almost invites a cross lines reply, while the second does not because it is an Adult one and could lead to a much better relationship between the two of you as well as better performance by both of you. From your subordinate's point of view, it could be a real demonstration of interest in him and a willingness to talk frankly. From your own point of view, it could mean that you would spend less of your time being burned up over such confrontations and, therefore, spend more of your time on creative activities.

Suppose you were just explaining some new work to one of the people working for you and he looked up and said, "Yeah, I guess it's all right, but I'm not sure. What about going all over it again?" If you replied, "The whole thing is pretty straightforward and quite simple; I don't see why you don't understand it unless you are just trying to give me the gears," what would be the reaction? Clearly, your reply shows a Parent ego state and is not likely to lead to a good relationship.

It doesn't always take words to show an ego state. Nonverbal responses can indicate them as well. If a response to a statement or some act is just a heavy sigh, the ego state is obviously that of a Parent. Similarly with head wagging, arms akimbo or maybe folded, and lips pursed. A Child state could be shown by anything from tears to squealing and squirming, shoulder shrugging, or even pouting. It is difficult to describe a nonverbal expression of an Adult state except to note that it is not one of the obvious Parent or Child ones.

LEADERSHIP

Now that we have looked at some of the basic aspects of human beings in general and individually, particularly in the organizational setting, we can discuss an important aspect of management: leadership. We will be dealing with this topic also in other places.

Although leadership is a well-accepted word in society, it is worthwhile to define it as it is being used here. Leadership as defined by Paul Hersey and Kenneth Blanchard in their book *Management of Organizational Behavior: Utilizing Human Resources* * is a "process of influencing the activities of an individual or a group in efforts toward accomplishing goals in a given situation."

In ancient days, leadership meant knowing what one wished to be done and then telling the people to do it. In this slave or feudal society, people, as we have already noted, were simply replaceable parts and were pushed and threatened with punishment in order to get them to do jobs. Probably even then, there were some leaders who did not use force all the time, as there were followers so sold on the leader's ideas that they did willingly what they were told to do.

Managerial Leadership

In reality we should place an adjective in front of the word leadership each time we use it here. That adjective is *managerial*. There are various kinds of leadership in our world. An actor or an artist may be a leader in his profession, but we are talking of a different meaning of the word leadership. A man or woman may be a political leader or a leader in a church or a social club. Again, this is different from managerial leadership. Unfortunately, the difference is glossed over many times, and some research on leadership has been done with social groups and the conclusions drawn have been transferred to paid-work organizations.

In social or political associations, the leaders are accountable to their followers. They represent their followers in the same way

*Englewood Cliffs, N.J.: Prentice-Hall, 1972, p. 68.

trade union leaders represent the members of their local. In either case, they report to their members or followers. A manager does not represent his subordinates in the same way. He can certainly get their views, and in order to maintain good working relationships, this is an essential requirement. However, he does not report back to them for their approval. He is accountable to the organization for which he works, and that means he is accountable to those above him. He can and does delegate responsibilities to those working for him, but he cannot transfer any of his accountability.

In the first part of this book we looked at what were referred to as the minimum responsibilities of a manager. Let us repeat them here, for they are very vital to our practicing of leadership in work organizations (how we may practice it in a church group is another matter). The four items we listed are:

- The right to hire those working for him or to veto a selection.
- The right to assign work tasks to people as he sees fit.
- The right to reward (or punish) subordinates within organizational policies.
- The right to fire a subordinate or move him to another spot in the organization.

If we accept these minimum items, then we have to think of managerial leadership as that which encourages and ensures the natural and enhanced motivation of people in order to get work done effectively. The manager is not the chairman of a committee of his workers who meet to make decisions. He seeks out ideas and participation for two basic reasons: (1) to develop a cohesive feeling among those who work for him, and (2) to discover new and useful suggestions for doing things. The decisions made are his decisions and not necessarily consensus ones. We must bear these differences about various types of leadership in mind as we go deeper into a discussion of this topic and leadership styles.

In our modern Western society, followers sometimes do things out of tremendous regard for their leaders, but this is not the case in the average organization. In most organizations, even the threat of violence or death does not succeed in getting work done. Now how do we apply the things we have learned so far about human beings?

In the last few decades several investigators have tried to find out what leadership qualities make a good manager. Various items were studied, from intelligence to perseverance, from sociability to magnetic dominance, from will power to strong achievement needs, among many others. The results of these studies pointed in no particular direction, possibly because different situations require different types of leadership, as do different times in the history of an organization or a country.

Many an inspiring wartime leader has found that the qualities that made him a success during wartime do not do so in peacetime, at least not generally. The whole emphasis on winning, which exists to a high degree in wartime, is rarely duplicated in peacetime. A small company with its back to the wall might use Army methods. Most others or government organizations cannot. Strangely, some military qualities are still preserved in associations of people who do social service or in political parties. And without pay as well. The answer is probably because they are fully sold on what they are doing or know there will be a personal political payoff in the future.

Two Aspects of Managerial Leadership

The basic studies examining leadership style—and this is important to success—looked at the two aspects of getting work done in the modern Western world. The first is the slave driver's need to get work done. The second is getting people to do the required work without using slavery techniques or those of a feudal or fascist society—or for that matter those of all early capitalist societies.

An early British industrialist and reformer, Robert Owen, wrote extensively some 150 years ago about the necessity of considering the needs of human beings in the workplace as thoroughly as one considered machinery and methods of production. As an industrialist himself, he used this approach to people and production in his New Lanark Mills in Scotland, and was an ardent crusader for human rights in the workplace. In a volume which gives his whole approach to a more human and rational society he wrote:

> These societies, being always supplied with the latest and best machinery for performing whatever it can be made to well execute, produce the greatest amount of the most valuable wealth in the shortest time and best manner and so as to produce health and enjoyment to all while engaged in . . . production.*

Much work has been done in trying to measure a manager's style as represented by his interest in getting the work done and in working with his people so they work at their tasks with positive attitudes. Various questionnaires are used, based on the work of Maslow, McGregor, and many others, particularly the Ohio State Center for Leadership Studies. What we are calling the manager's interest in getting the work done, the Ohio researchers defined more rigidly as the _task behavior_ of the manager, while what we referred to as working with people to get the tasks done, they called his _relationship behavior_.

Task behavior means that a manager gives a clear description of the tasks to be done, the activities required to accomplish the tasks, and the roles of all involved in performing these activities and where and when these tasks are to be carried out. All this, of course, is tied to the operating framework of the organization, including its styles of communication and methods of doing things.

Relationship behavior means that a manager relates to his subordinates as personal individuals and also as groups, helping them psychologically to do the tasks and having good interpersonal relations as well as ability to facilitate task accomplishment by his people.

At one time these two types of behavior were thought to be at

* Robert Owen, _The Book of the New Moral World_, first published by The Home Colonization Society, London, 1842, and reprinted by Augustus M. Kelley, New York, 1970.

the opposite ends of a continuum, with each manager showing up somewhere along the line between the two extremes. However, it soon became clear that each manager probably had some elements of both in his makeup, and therefore his style had to be thought of in terms of a mixture of both.

The Managerial Grid®

One of the best-known and most widely used questionnaires is the Managerial Grid®, which is based on the work of Robert Blake and Jane Mouton. The grid they developed identifies and brings into focus a number of theories of managerial behavior. These are based on our two fundamental variable factors: management concern for production (output) and management concern for people (the quality of interpersonal relations). In the context of the grid, the phrase "concern for production" is not meant to indicate how much production is obtained, nor is concern for people intended to reflect the degree to which human relations needs actually are met. The emphasis is rather on the *degree* of "concern for," because action is rooted in basic attitudes. What is significant is how much a supervisor is concerned about production and how much about human relationships.

The words "production" and "human relationships" cover a range of considerations. Production is not limited to things. Its proper meaning covers whatever it is that people are engaged in accomplishing. In a similar fashion, human aspects of interaction cover a variety of different concerns. Included are concern for the degree of personal commitment to completing a job for which one is responsible, personal accountability based on trust rather than force, self-esteem of an individual, desire for a sense of security in work, work and social relations with coworkers, and many other similar concerns.

The Managerial Grid® (see Figure 4) attempts to summarize these two concerns and the possible interactions between them. The horizontal axis indicates concern for production, while the vertical axis indicates concern for people. Each is expressed in a nine-point scale.

Figure 4. The Managerial Grid.® (From *The New Managerial Grid* by Robert R. Blake and Jane Srygley Mouton. Houston: Gulf Publishing Company,©1978, page II. Reproduced by permission.)

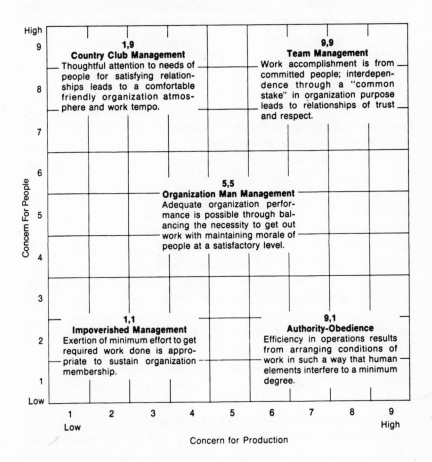

Although there are many managerial theories that may be shown on this grid, emphasis is usually placed on the four corner points (1.1, 9.9, 1.9, and 9.1—and the mid-point, 5.5). These positions are seldom found in pure form, but they make clear-cut examples to discuss, and there are some situations that approach rather closely one or the other of these positions.

At the lower left corner of the grid is the 1.1 style, where there is a minimum of both concern for production and concern for people. This is described as impoverished management, where effective production is unobtainable because managers believe people are lazy, apathetic, or indifferent. Sound and mature interpersonal relationships are difficult to achieve, and conflict is inevitable.

The 1.9 style in the upper left corner represents maximum concern for people but minimum concern for production. This is described as "country club management," where much thoughtful attention is given to the needs of people. It is held that this would lead to satisfying relationships that provide a comfortable friendly atmosphere and work tempo. Although conflict is much reduced, production may suffer.

The 9.1 style in the lower right portrays maximum concern for production and minimum concern for human relationships. The resulting style is "task management," where efficiency in operations results from arranging conditions of work in such a way that human relationships interfere as little as possible. People are a commodity, just like machines. A manager's responsibility is considered to be to plan, direct, and control the work of those subordinate to him. It is evident that in most organizations this sort of management style is much more prevalent than the 1.9 or the 1.1 styles.

The 9.9 style in the upper right hand corner represents maximum concern for both human relationships and production. This is management where work accomplishment comes from committed people. The interdependence of people through a "common stake" in organization purpose generates relationships of trust and respect.

The 5.5 style in the center of the diagram is "middle of the road" in both areas of concern. An adequate organization performance is possible through balancing the necessity to get out work while maintaining the morale of people at a satisfactory level. The manager would push for production but not go all out. He should be fair but firm with his subordinates.

Managers Have More Than One Style

Probably very few people consistently use one style. In analyzing styles on their grid, Blake and Mouton allow for one or more backup styles. These later, though not dominant, may be used from time to time depending on the circumstances. Despite the idea of trying to be effective in your own style, provided it is not in the undesirable poor area of the grid, most managers feel they should be aiming for the 9.9 style of management.

McGregor has pointed out that a manager can effectively change his style without changing his basic values and ideas. If his perception of himself changes, then how he acts as a manager, and indeed in general, can very well change too. We have seen before that we act by our perceptions of reality and not by the realities seen by others. Seeing ourselves as others see us can be of great help, and this is one of the values of such questionnaires as that of Blake and Mouton.

William Reddin* has been concerned with the quality of effectiveness added to such a grid as the Managerial Grid®. He believes that certain styles are more effective under varying conditions and that a manager should be well aware of this. Reddin has devised what amounts to a three-dimensional grid, with effectiveness being the added axis. He thus separates his ideas into eight basic styles, which he claims are equally distributed throughout management.

Reddin lists four more-effective styles and four less-effective ones. A person with high concern for getting a job done and low interest in the people side of it is a benevolent autocrat in a situation where this style—for some reason or other—is appropriate and, therefore, effective. When the situation isn't appropriate, then he becomes less effective and is labeled an autocrat. A parallel, mentioned earlier, might be the wartime style of leadership not being effective in peacetime.

*Management Style Diagnosis Test, Fredericton, New Brunswick, Canada: Organizational Tests, Ltd., 1972.

Finding the Effective Style

The question arises, how do you know when one style is effective or not? The situation tells you, but how? And how adaptable does a manager have to be? In reference to the last point, a good manager has to be very adaptable, since he must change styles to fit changing situations.

A good answer to all this comes out of the prolonged studies at the Center for Leadership Studies at Ohio State. The theory resulting from these studies is called the life cycle theory of leadership and is based on the idea that a person matures in the performance of specific tasks and that this maturing process calls for changes in leadership style. A person may not mature in all his tasks, so the style has to be adapted to performance on each specific task. This idea has been developed by Hersey and Blanchard, and has been referred to as situational leadership.*

At a low level of maturity in a task, so the idea goes, a manager should use more of a task orientation in his dealing with that person regarding that specific task. As the individual becomes more adept at the task and can accomplish it better, the style should become more people centered, using positive recognition of progress, even if slow, as a means of reinforcing the maturing ability.

This adds a whole new dimension to leadership style, as it suggests that a 9.9 style in the Managerial Grid System® is not always the most effective one, or that a Theory X approach is not always the least effective one. In other words, the style of the manager is not always the key to his success. He requires the ability to analyze the situation involving those he works with and adapt his style to the individual maturity of the worker on that specific task at that time. The manager must also bear in mind that maturity, even bolstered by recognition of progress, is not always a growing thing. Personal emotional crises can easily set an individual back.

*Paul Hersey and Ken Blanchard, *Management of Organizational Behavior: Utilizing Human Resources,* 3rd ed. (Englewood Cliffs, N.J.: Prentice-Hall, 1977).

At least two other items should be borne in mind when utilizing this approach. The first is that the cultural background of an individual influences his or her perception of a worker–boss relationship and often requires a more task-centered approach, even though the individual may be capable of doing a specific task. People brought up in a more authoritarian culture with more sharply drawn class relationships may demand stricter task-orientation on the part of the manager.

Some years ago a psychologist friend of mine, who was very concerned with the cooperative approach to organizational work and was very active in his community, became engaged in building a cultural hall for the community. Never having been in an actual management position before, he was delighted with the opportunity of practicing what he had been preaching. When construction was to start and the ground was strewn with equipment and materials for the job, he called a group of workmen over. He showed them the basic plans for the building and said that they were all working together to build the community hall. The workmen were normal construction workers living in the area.

The psychologist felt very good when he talked about cooperation in doing the job. The workmen smiled at him. Little work was accomplished. My friend thought that he hadn't made himself clear enough and decided to tackle the situation again. He even used a translator to make sure that what he said was correctly understood by the workers, who were mainly recent Italian immigrants. They were happy people but still weren't clear about what was going on.

Little work was still being done. Finally my friend got a little raw around the nerve edges. He started to get specific about who was to dig where, who was to work with concrete and bricks, even who was to carry the bricks, and so on. He went into some detail about the first jobs to be done to build the hall, things he considered obvious to all. But he was mad. Even without the benefit of translation, a look of comprehension came over the workers. "Boss," several said, "now we know what you want us to do. Sure we will do it." And the work got going and everyone was happy.

author

What the psychologist had forgotten, for all his learning, was that the workers were mainly fresh from Southern Italy or Sicily and were used to a culture in which they were told what to do. They were not asked to group together and cooperate in achieving a common aim. They were simply given orders, and they carried them out. That was the standard procedure to them at that time. My friend had used the wrong kind of leadership and got nowhere with his first approach.

motives

The second item we should be concerned with deals with motives of each individual as we discussed these when talking about achievement, power, and affiliation. Those with a very high achievement drive tend to be more intolerant of a task-centered approach, particularly in tasks where a growth of innovative ideas is desirable, as in commissioned salespeople, for example.

Salesmen have strong achievement drives and do not like to complete a lot of paperwork, whereas people with strong affiliation drives can be happy filling in a variety of forms. A manager must be aware of what style to use in each of these cases. A task-centered approach to form filling by salesmen will rarely succeed over time, and different methods have to be developed to obtain the required information. Maturity is also not as simple a development as it might appear to be. Many workers only desire to mature at a task until they are doing it as well and as fast as the average person in their group. In these cases, the manager often has to resort to a more task-centered approach when theory first indicates that he should use a people-centered one.

The value of the life cycle theory of leadership is that it gets away from the unitary theme implicit in the minds of people when they hear about Theory X and Theory Y or the 9.9 classification of the Managerial Grid®. It describes managers for what more of them are in practice, namely, adaptable. It gets them to improve their adaptability rather than strive for the rigidity of a 9.9 approach or a 1.9 one, for that matter.

Though certain styles are thought to be more effective in certain situations, there are still some qualities of a real manager that appear to make for an effective operation in general. These separate a person who has a capacity for management work from those who have little or no capacity for management work. Undoubtedly there are people who never should become managers, because they do not have any of the abilities required. Those who have the qualities for effective management can utilize various styles of management, depending on the situation. It is interesting and instructive to contrast the qualities of effective and ineffective managers in general, as done below.

Qualities of an Effective Manager

• Has good understanding of knowledge and skills required by his immediate subordinates. Sets tasks and general responsibilities in a manner clear to his subordinates and ones which he feels they have the ability to carry out.
• Places emphasis on task-oriented roles. Shows how the immediate activities are related to others performed in the firm.
• Allows a free exchange of different opinions and is very willing to discuss differences as well as items not fully understood.
• Tries to discover how people are thinking and why.
• Has respect for all opinions and doesn't laugh at any which may be advanced. Can change his own mind.
• Makes decisions personally, and with enthusiasm, after discussions. Doesn't require full consensus for his decisions.
• Sees problems ahead and seeks ways to solve them as well as work on immediate problem areas. Doesn't allow current problems to drag on.
• Accepts the blame when things go wrong with his operations.

Qualities of an Ineffective Manager

• Has poor understanding of knowledge and skills required by his immediate subordinates. Assigns tasks without real knowledge of individual's abilities to tackle them.
• Either runs at problems or solves them without giving the facts of the situation much consideration. If he doesn't find some solution, allows a problem to fester over too long a time.
• Is up and down in personal feelings. When he rushes through a

problem and finds a solution acceptable to him, will not reconsider it under almost any circumstances.

- Relies on strict enforcement of his and other rules to run his operation and insists this is best for all concerned.
- Feels physically ill about things which happen at times.
- Doesn't stick to tasks and keeping things moving.
- Permits group to make decisions and then blames them if they don't work out.
- Compromises too much and believes this solves problems.
- Blames senior managers for his difficulties and problems in order to take load off his back.

CREATIVE MANAGEMENT

Good management has to be creative in two main areas: first, in logically analyzing the needs of the organization so that its objectives are well worked out and the sequencing of all its operations intelligently thought through; second, in working with all employees to see that they contribute as much as they can to fulfill the objectives.

These two items can reinforce each other as well as oppose each other. To dovetail them properly and continuously is always a challenge. Because people are individuals and situations—as well as the mix of employees—change, the tasks are rarely carried out fully successfully over time. A good manager is aware that he is living in a flux of forces aimed at completing objectives. As with growing crops, there is a continuous need to have fertilizers and antidotes against diseases and other crop destroyers. This is the nature of the managerial job, and any person who expects to someday obtain full calm and 100 percent success should think of another occupation. Does any one offer that?

The manager, then, has to be aware of the fundamentals of an organization created to achieve objectives—and these never stand still either—as well as the fundamentals of working in harmony with people, both above and below him. He then has to make the decisions on an individual basis. There is no cookbook approach to solving each problem as it occurs. There is only an understanding reinforced by experience and the work capacity of the individual. Capable managers develop intuition—some kind of gut feeling—that can serve them in good stead and can even be a main bulwark against doing the wrong things. This attitude toward unexpressable ideas inside him which ring warning bells or give green lights should be akin to what the great musician Pablo Casals said about music in his autobiography *Joys and Sorrows:*

> It has always been my viewpoint that intuition is the decisive element in both the composing and the performance of music. Of course technique and intelligence have vital functions—one must master the techniques of an instrument in order to exact its full potentialities and one must apply one's intelligence in exploring every facet of the music—but, ultimately, the paramount role is that of intuition. For me the determining factor in creativity, in bringing a work to life, is that of musical instinct.*

We may be presumptuous in putting management in league with music creation, but there are many parallels. We can teach some of the basics, and might inspire diligent practice of these basic skills in the work situation, but ultimately all we can hope for is that many who learn and practice the basics will develop the intuition of an excellent manager. But never forget to keep studying the basics and practicing them—as any good musician does—not only to keep the instincts alive, but to enhance them.

Questions for Review

(Use extra paper when required.)

1. Describe the three ego states of people and give some information on how they evolve.

_____

_____

_____

_____

*Pablo Casals, as told to Albert F. Kahn. New York: Simon & Schuster, 1970, p. 97.

2. In the following examples, give the ego state shown by the responses (use P, A, and C in the boxes on the right).

A subordinate tells his manager: "There have been all sorts of promises since I came here, but very little delivery. Am I supposed to believe what you say now?"

Answer A: "I don't recall ever really breaking a promise to ☐ you. I would like to know your side. We had better talk this over right away."

Answer B: "If I seemed to let you down there was a good ☐ reason. Just go along now and you'll see my word is as good as my bond."

Answer C: "Don't always drag up the past. That's a sore ☐ loser attitude. What we're talking about is a big deal, so hang in."

A confrere says to a fellow manager: "Hell, no one wants to say yes or no about anything. Why can't we get some straight answers once in a while?"

Reply A: "If it involves me, I make decisions. Give me a ☐ shout next time you can't get a reply. Two to one I'll straighten it out."

Reply B: "Did you just bump against old Nick again, or are ☐ you getting the 'maybe' treatment from all sides?"

Reply C: "Do you expect that crew upstairs to change at all? ☐ At least if they don't tell us what's up, they can't blame us when things are down."

A subordinate says to his boss: "That idea really throws me. It sounds a little on the unethical side. What should I do?"

Answer A: "You have to ask me that? Just make yourself look ☐ good. That is all you can really do about it."

Answer B: "Think it over carefully first and then, if you wish ☐ me to help you make up your mind, let me know."

Answer C: "I'm surprised they mentioned that; it does sound ☐ a little off. Just do what you feel like about it and the hell with it."

3. List the five key styles of managers as developed in the Managerial Grid® and some basic information about each one.

_____

_____

_____

_____

4. From your own knowledge or experience, describe an incident where a manager used an ineffective style. Explain the circumstances and indicate what style you think might have been more effective.

_____

_____

_____

_____

5. Describe the main ingredients of the situational theory of leadership.

_____

_____

_____

_____

6. What are some difficulties you can see in making use of this theory?

_____

_____

_____

_____

7. From your knowledge or experience, describe some good and/or bad uses of intuition by managers.

_____

_____

_____

_____

8. What is the relationship of intuition to luck?

_____

_____

_____

Case Study
Hannaby and Rogers

Charles William Browning is a man around 30 years of age who had studied to be a lawyer himself but had never finished his first year. He then decided to study accounting and took a number of courses. His grades were good, as were the ones he achieved while in law school. However, he got married and became a father and decided to stop his studies and get a job. He obtained one as an assistant in a small accounting firm and a year and a half later heard of an opening in Hannaby and Rogers as a member of the office staff. He applied for the job and received it.

He was considered to be a good worker, and several of the lawyers in the firm encouraged him to finish his legal studies. He said that he was going to do so but never got started. After a few months' employment he was heard to make caustic remarks about some of the people in the office, commenting on how things were done and how they should be carried on. Roger Pillbody, the office manager, spoke to him, and Browning was very apologetic and said that he meant no harm and had been misconstrued.

For a few months all was fairly quiet and Browning did a satisfactory job. Then he was heard to criticize some of the legal members of the firm and talk about his own training and what he would have done in their position. Billwell Hannaby, the senior partner, spoke to him after a few complaints about his behavior. Browning cosied up to the senior, saying that he was not criticizing people who knew better than he did, that he had talked about some of the cases and given his own opinion, but that these were not really criticisms. Hannaby advised him to watch what he said, pointing out that although some of the juniors did not always do the right thing, it was not the job of an office person to discuss their work. Hannaby again suggested that if Browning continued his own studies, there might be a place for him on the legal staff of the firm.

A few months later, on the telephone to a new client, Browning pretended to be a legal member of the firm and gave his opinion. A few days later the same client spoke to Hannaby and thanked him for the advice given by the employee. Hannaby was disturbed but said nothing to the client.

Guide Questions

1. What do you think of the leadership given by Billwell Hannaby to Charles Browning?
2. How should Hannaby have handled Browning on his various interviews?
3. What should the firm do to improve control in its office?
4. What should be done now with Browning?

CHAPTER 3

Planning

In Chapter 1 we referred briefly to five major functions of management. These were planning, organizing, staffing, directing, and controlling. We will be using these five as a framework in order to discuss the activities which managers engage in to get their work done. These activities will include such practical items as goal setting, decision making, recruiting, counseling, appraising people, training people, and generally setting priorities and accomplishing work within the allotted time.

We have mentioned five functions here. There is no full agreement among people interested in management theory about exactly how many functions there are and what they are. Some leave out staffing as a major function, some use leading instead of directing, some break the functions in other ways. You will find some different ways of stating the functions if you leaf through a number of books. We should not worry too much about the names used but about the activities involved in carrying out the work of managers.

FAYOL'S FIVE FUNCTIONS OF MANAGEMENT

It is rather interesting that one of the first persons to spell out the work of the manager as an overall general task of all managers used just about the same names as the five above, allowing for some liberties in translating and modernizing the terms. He was a very active French senior manager by the name of Henri Fayol who, in 1916, on the basis of his life work and interest, produced a small volume titled *Administration industrielle et générale*. A good deal of Fayol's management activities took place during the same time that Frederick Taylor was operating in the United States. Fayol's ideas did not become known to many of us, because he wrote in French. There was no full translation of his book into English until 1949.

We will briefly describe Fayol's ideas of the functions here, because they are still very much in line with modern concepts, and they serve as a good starting place for the next sections.

Planning—the activities which shape the future direction of the organization and develop the actions necessary to accomplish the selected goals.

Organizing—the selection and assignment of the tasks to be performed in an orderly and logical fashion, including the structure and relationships required to tackle the tasks.

Staffing—obtaining the individuals required to staff the positions, allowing for some personal initiative and ensuring good rapport between the organization and its employees.

Directing—helping people reach the organization's goals through clear and fair agreements and good superiors who are able to handle the agreements with integrity and authority.

Controlling—checking progress against the plans and determining what changes must be made if expected results are not being achieved.

There may be some confusion in the minds of some because in discussing the functions of management, we have not mentioned such things as manufacturing, marketing, and financing. These are often considered to be the functions of managers. In reality they are the functions of the organization rather than of management. In many organizations manufacturing is not performed; marketing, which is based on satisfying customers' needs for products and services and/or selling them, varies a great deal in many organizations; financing, which is expressing plans in dollar terms and keeping the accounts and is, therefore, a major tool in planning and controlling, is all pervasive in organizations but varies from place to place.

The functions of planning, organizing, staffing, directing, and controlling are essential to the operation of the marketing department and the manufacturing department as well as to the business in general. They are common essential ingredients of all organizations from hospitals to wire wheel makers.

PLANNING

In this section we will take a broad look at the overall planning process of an organization but not go into details of top management planning. We will indicate the major parts and activities involved, because they are pertinent to the operation of all organizations, and we will examine their implications for the various departments of the organization. This will lead to a discussion of problem solving and decision making, which are critical to achieving the goals and objectives of an organization. Finally, we shall look at setting priorities and timing activities—sometimes referred to as time management—which is an area of major importance to all aspects of planning.

Some wise person once said that if you don't know where you are going, there are a million paths for you to take for your journey. In a similar way, if you don't know what you are trying to accomplish, there are a million methods to select from. Simple truths, perhaps, but thousands of organizations exist today with still only a half worked-out idea of where they are going and what they are trying to do. Executives who feel their objectives are well enough known without having to be written down would be surprised how much difficulty they would have if they tried to write them down. If they wrote down their objectives, they would also find their thinking clearer in case objectives have to be changed. In days gone by, the unwritten rule was probably good enough. Changes came slowly and did not demand clarity of objectives. Today change is planned, change is perpetual, speedy change is the way of life. Clarity of objectives becomes more and more essential if organizations are to function effectively. A slow-flying plane of the early days could flutter around until it found the place it was looking for. A jet must know its objective clearly and proceed there with a plan, otherwise it might discharge passengers at London instead of Vancouver.

Objectives and Boundaries

In any discussion of the planning work of managers in organizations, we have to start with two basic considerations: (1) the purpose, goals, and/or objectives of the organization, and (2) the parameters or boundaries of the organization. The second might be considered as part of the first. However, it is useful to look at the two items separately.

The word organization rather than business is used here, because the basic ideas to be discussed are relevant to any organization of people, whether it is a business or a government department. Jargons may differ and approaches may differ; these only reflect the complexity of the subject. The basic concepts underlying the management of any organization are the same.

To prevent confusion we should add a most vital side note. In our text we are always talking about a work organization, not an association of people such as those who form political parties or skiing clubs. What we are discussing in this text could refer to the paid work staff of a political party or ski club, but not to the voluntary membership in each. There are certain basic differences between these two types of groupings; the word organization is, unfortunately, used to mean voluntary social, political, and cultural groupings as well as paid work forces set up to carry out objectives, whether for profit or otherwise.

The main reason for examining the purpose or purposes of an organization is to concentrate on what the organization is trying to accomplish and thus lead to a clarification of its goals. In practice this is a never-ending process. Another major reason for being concerned with what many people may think of as obvious is to make sure that main opportunities are discerned and acted upon. Often, organizations simply carry on with what they are doing and try to improve their activities. They may be missing the boat. That was literally true for many boat builders not so long ago. They were so concerned with improving their cargo vessels to operate faster and better at sea that they forgot that the name of the game was becoming turnaround time in port! Then, when this was realized, container vessels and container ports became popular.

Any organization is a complicated system of interactions between people working at various levels in that organization and reacting with the social, economic, cultural, political, and competitive systems which surround it. From this modern viewpoint, we can see that both the parameters of the organization and its objectives must be clearly known if it is to be effectively operated. This does not prevent parameters and objectives from changing over the years.

The Parameters of an Organization

People often talk about the old railway systems, particularly those in the United States. They considered themselves as steam railways and were not alive to the fact that transportation in general, and even opening up the countryside, was their business. Their parameters were tightly drawn over a hundred years ago, and many managers did not see the need to change them as other means of transportation came into being, nor did they see that even their role in transportation was changing; they were losing passengers but building up cheap freight. The result was bankruptcy for many firms.

It is interesting that there was a similarity between this and an airline in recent history. World War I ace pilot Eddie Rickenbacker built Eastern Airlines. He was obviously a brilliant individualist and made a tremendous firm of Eastern in the early days. The firm was described by one who worked for Rickenbacker as "a masterpiece of piston technology and thinking." Came the jets and the short hops connecting cities in the Eastern United States were too short; the new aircraft were also taking people farther and farther away in the same time that Eastern could take them on short hops. The company began to crumble. It had no written objectives, no useful organizational setup, no preventative maintenance policy, and so forth. Like the railroads, it became a victim of circumscribed parameters and lack of spelled-out objectives. In our fast-moving society, Eastern was headed for the dumps in much less time than it took the railroads of another age to do so. Fortunately, Eastern's plight was attended to at the eleventh hour. Times change, but some management thinking does not.

Scott Seed once called on Peter Drucker, eminent management consultant, and requested his advice on the general functioning of the firm. The company made grass seed. In examining this case, Drucker looked not only at how the firm functioned but also at the environment in which it functioned. When he finished his investigation, he told them their job was not selling grass seeds but good lawns. This is what the customer was after. He suggested that the firm market good lawns, and this meant selling fertilizers, pesticides, advice on how to grow the best lawn for specific soil conditions, and so on. Thus the boundaries of the firm were changed, not just the workings of the part which was Scott Seed in the beginning.

A statement of what a business is and should be may sound rather ridiculous, but thinking of it can be helpful. A man may go into business to sell solid wooden house doors, and he may do a fair, if somewhat small, business. If he decided not to limit himself to solid doors but also to sell hollow-core and other types of doors and throw in door hardware, such as hinges and handles, he would make his business more viable. He might even go in for windows as well, figuring that his business was materials and fittings for house openings. He might even branch into commercial doors.

If this sort of statement still sounds farfetched, just think back to days not too long ago when lumber firms were ranting at building material suppliers who offered not only lumber for sale but all types of building supplies, some of which were in competition with lumber. The problem was that most buyers of lumber were really looking for building materials and tools, and the alert merchant who set out to satisfy this need made profits, much to the disgust of the old conservative "lumber-is-sacred" dealers.

We have focused on business firms here, because they may be easier to examine from the point of view of objectives and parameters. However, the same thinking applies to government organizations and other non-business ones. Reorganizations take place from time to time in order to meet new objectives. Giving people in need food and lodging—once the be-all and end-all of many of our social service organizations—has considerably broadened as the meaning of needed services to people was examined in the light of our changing world.

Areas for Setting Objectives

In his book *The Practice of Management* Peter Drucker states that there are eight areas for setting objectives.* Drucker is basically concerned with business organizations, but his thinking can be extended to other organizations as well. The eight, with added comments, are:

1. *Market standing.* The interest here is with the size of the market and the full potential of it, the share for the company, the size and quality of the sales force, as well as the quality of the product or service. Price and advertising also should be questioned. Some of this is not the concern of a service organization, although many of them are trying to look at their clients as their customers and should be concerned whether or not they are reaching the people they should be and serving them with highest quality of service.

2. *Innovation.* This is concerned with the development of new and better products and services. Drucker's claim was that the highest profits come with innovative products and services. To the leader go a lot of the spoils. The "me-too" companies rarely make as much as the innovators. He realizes that innovation can gener-

*New York: Harper & Row, 1954.

ally only be a minor part of company activities, but a very important part. There can also be innovations in marketing and pricing. The question of innovative services in the public sector is just as important as in the private sector, and there is no doubt about the need for innovative marketing in public organizations.

3. *Productivity.* The interest here is with output per worker, sales per salesman, output per dollar of investment, and so on. Productivity has been of major concern to people in all organizations, and ways to increase it without using threats is a top priority.

4. *Physical and financial resources.* This is concerned with looking at the specifics of obtaining and developing the resources required to keep an organization in operation.

5. *Profitability.* In a company, this can be specified as an intention to achieve a certain return on the dollar, on net assets, or on gross sales.

6. *Manager performance and development.* Actually, performance and development can be looked at as starting with the lowest manager and going right to the top. How do we improve conditions, both physical and emotional, in an organization in order to influence the motivation of people positively? We have looked at many ideas about this in past chapters. It must also be planned for. There is another aspect to this in a broad plan. If the goals of any organization are to change according to changing plans, then the types of personnel working for the organization have to be looked at fully as well. Plans must also be drawn up and implemented to make personnel fully acquainted with any changes to be made so they will be capable of functioning when these are implemented.

7. *Worker performance and attitude.* In the previous item we were concerned mainly with the managers in an organization. Here we are concerned with the bottom-level workers. In theory, both items might be incorporated into one; in practice, they seldom are, since worker performances often involve more specific skills development and relations with trade unions.

8. *Public responsibility.* Since the time Drucker spelled out his ideas on the areas of concern in setting objectives, this item has

become a very important one. Corporate affairs are being inked into many company's objectives, and they can no longer be—as they often were—mere verbal statements of concern by top management. Today, they figure in the dollars and cents operations of a growing number of companies. The same is true, possibly to a lesser extent at present, in public organizations.

Spelling Out the Broad Purpose

In a speech some years back when the then head office of Northern Telecom Inc. was spelling out its objectives, Vice President V. O. Marquez stated:

> One of the primary obligations of management at *all* levels is to define "purpose," because a clearly stated purpose provides a common criterion of value against which all activities can be measured. When a common purpose is available, for the company, for the department, the primary question to be resolved about any proposed action or decision is "does it serve the 'purpose' or does it not?" When the answer to this key question is "yes," there can be far greater flexibility in the choice of means and people are less likely to adopt a slavish adherence to uniformity, unnecessary routine, or traditional practice. . . .

> When purpose *is* clear and communicated as wisely and deeply as possible throughout all the people in an organization, among nonmanagement people as well as among managers, opportunities for the use of initiative, of creativity, of self-reliance, and of independent thinking multiply enormously.

> The fact is that it is the prerogative and the primary obligation of senior management to define purpose sharply and clearly with *no alternatives* but on the other hand to encourage and demand as wide a range as possible of alternatives in the *choice of means*. This is precisely the opposite of the way management is normally practiced in most companies.*

There is no one way to describe the ideas, but we prefer objectives, goals, and purposes because they sound more direct than

*From a speech delivered at a seminar, University of Toronto, 1964.

others. Objectives should also not be the exclusive property of top managers. They should filter all the way down to the bottom of the firm, with each subgroup or department working at its own objectives, in keeping with the overall ones of the organization. While stating objectives at top levels clearly accomplishes something, the real impact on the organization's activities only comes when objectives are understood all the way down.

Stating the parameters of an organization and its objectives is not a simple exercise. It cannot be tossed off in a short time. Each sentence must have meaning that can be expanded and reworded at lower levels. Each sentence must educate all in how to proceed, and no two statements should lead to conflicts in the minds of lower-level managers. Both boundaries and objectives must offer positive guides for action, and guides devoid of fat and fancy. The statements should also offer some challenge.

It is interesting to look at these ideas in the light of some thoughts expressed by the Committee for Economic Development on what qualities should be required for young managers. These were stated as qualities to be emphasized in the training of students in business schools and published in a report of the Committee. They are:

1. Analytical ability and balanced judgment.
2. The capacity to solve problems and reach decisions in a sound and well-organized manner.
3. Vigor of mind and imagination.
4. Understanding of human behavior and of social, political, and economic forces.
5. The ability to work with—and lead—others.
6. A character that assures adherence to high principles under stress.
7. The ability to keep an open mind and to continue learning on one's own initiative.

If these seem reasonable to most people, then it should be obvious that managers with these qualities would be more at home and much better able to function in an organization whose objectives are properly spelled out. Many of these qualities would be frustrated in an organization whose parameters and objectives are vague at best. True, there are other factors necessary in an organization for effective performance on the part of managers, but the objectives represent the taking-off point for all the others.

Proper spelling out of objectives at all levels goes hand in hand with good management. Though one could probably find examples that disprove this statement, further research into the details would probably reveal one or more of several conditions:

- Spelled-out objectives may not have been thought-out objectives first.
- Spelled-out objectives are not static, they must be reviewed and revised when necessary.
- Objectives may be clearly set in the mind of a top manager, particularly in a small business; if he communicates well, he may manage well, too.

All the functions of a manager require first knowing the parameters of a business and where it is heading. That is why we have stressed it so thoroughly.

Some Examples

Having said so much so far, let's look at how some companies spell out their goals or objectives. In its 1978 annual report, Wyle Laboratories set out the major goals for its Distribution Group. The long-range goal was to grow over 15 percent each year while maintaining a return on assets of 20 percent. For the coming year its immediate goals were:

1. Continue to grow faster than the electronics distribution industry.
2. Improve our profitability and asset turnover with major emphasis on inventory control.
3. Improve our planning for growth on the "Microprocessor Systems" business.

4. Improve our marketing organization and ability to plan programs with our suppliers.
5. Increase our emphasis on recruiting and training to keep pace with rapid growth.

The company got started in El Segundo in 1950, basically to provide testing services to the aircraft component manufacturers in southern California. Over the years it went into other associated businesses, of which the Wyle Distribution Group is its largest, in terms of sales.

The Alabama Bancorporation, in setting some goals for the same year, states that it plans to emphasize:

1. Increasing the growth rate of core deposits.
2. Expanding customer services which provide non-interest revenues.
3. Improving operating efficiency.
4. Continuing the improvement of our methods of selection, training, and compensating our personnel.

The 1978 goals of these two companies are expressed in fairly general terms, although Wyle does have some long-range goals that are set out in numbers. Obviously the more general type of goal has to be expressed in numbers for strategic purposes, otherwise no specific plans could be developed and actions organized to accomplish them. There would be no real way of measuring success. The numbers used by these firms would be expressed in plans which are kept private.

Like the long-range goals stated in percentages by Wyle, the Dennison Manufacturing Company, a firm with products ranging from school supplies to word processing systems, has four performance goals for itself. It measures its success each year on the basis of how well it does. These goals are:

1. Return on opening equity to exceed 15 percent.
2. Return on sales to exceed 5 percent.
3. Sales growth of 10 percent in real terms annually.
4. Increase regular dividend by 10 percent.

The goals do not tell anything about what the objectives are in each of the product areas where it operates. Some firms spell out publicly both general and strategic goals, but most do not reveal all. The full statement of goals, on which the plans are based, are kept under wraps. Here's how another firm mixes in general and strategic goals, but still does not reveal all:

- To utilize the assets of the corporation in the most effective manner to increase total sales and profits.
- To increase sales at the rate of 20 percent per year for the next five years.
- To realize a minimum return on investment of 15 percent after taxes.
- To have commercial sales and profits at least equal to military sales and profits.
- To have at least 50 percent of our business in the sale of standard products.
- To spend up to 5 percent of our income on the development of new standard products to sustain and improve the existing businesses.
- To seek sensible diversification through outside acquisition.
- To develop a strong organization to operate existing businesses with sufficient depth to assure business continuity and to provide management for new acquisitions.
- To recognize the importance of "ability to market" and "cost of marketing" when evaluating opportunities for new-products development or outside acquisitions.
- To seek good relations with the public, the financial community, our stockholders, and our customers; and to win and hold the respect of our employees.
- To recognize the different characteristics of different kinds of business; and to find the most effective and efficient method of operating each different business that we undertake.

Questions to Ask in Planning

In none of the examples just discussed does the company provide a complete statement of objectives. They do not discuss the primary question, except indirectly, of what is the nature or purpose of their organization. Possibly the best way to get a full flavor of what goes on in the process is to list some general questions that should be asked when an organization reviews its purpose and its parameters. The questions tend to look simple, but they do dig deep when gone into. Their simplicity leads people to dismiss them as a mental exercise, but only a small organization can afford to keep the answers buried somewhere in its managers' heads.

Worked out, written-down planning is crucial to success. Unfortunately it takes time, and with the many other activities of any organization, it can be shunted aside. If tackled properly and with conviction, it need not take that much time. Alfred Sloan's original plan for General Motors when he became president in 1921 took him only a few weeks, yet it changed the firm from an also ran to the giant Ford Company to the biggest in its field within a short span of time.

What are these questions to ask when planning?

1. *Where are we?* What is the nature of our organization? What is the basic knowledge of our organization? Businessmen might ask, what business are we really in? Not too long ago when office-type copiers were being developed, printers were offered the idea. They dismissed it without much thought, for it wasn't really "printing" and, therefore, not considered competitive to the printers. To their dismay, they later learned that the new reproduction materials took a lot of business away from them. It was almost a repetition of the time when the first linotype machines were not considered useful for the printing industry. Then they took over and had their day. That day passed, but the old attitude didn't. It represented the same failure to ask: what really is our business? What is our basic knowledge?

Other questions that belong here are: How did we obtain our best results? and our poorest? What were the reasons for our successes and our failures? People? products or services? facilities? ready cash? or a mixture of some or all of these? Do we have products, services, or ideas whose day is past but we are not yet aware of this and are spending precious time and money on them?

2. *What is our past?* How has the nature of the organization changed? What things did we drop? What new things did we adopt

that led us to our present position? What were our fears which didn't materialize? What basic ideas and policies have remained unchanged and helped us get to our current status?

3. *What is our future?* What is the forecast for the future? What assumptions should we make about our world regarding wars, major shifts in trade and technology and governments? Will there be more interrelationships with other bodies, such as governments and consumer and other associations? Will attitudes change toward material possessions? Toward working?

What is the general economic outlook? What is the outlook for our particular interests? What does marketing research reveal about the future? What opportunities will be open to use? Where can we innovate?

4. *How do we get there?* What happens if we make no basic changes? What changes appear essential, in our organizational setup, in the mix of people we need, in the training and development of our people and the hiring of others to do our work? What is the effect of such changes on our finances and financing? What risks can we take?

The next step is to convert the insights achieved from the answers to these questions into effective planning—that is, to develop a strategic plan. The strategic plan will include the following elements:

An order of priorities.

A sequencing and timing of events.

A breakdown into departmental objectives.

A breakdown into requirements of materials, equipment, and people and matching against current resources.

Drawing up, if required, of new policies, procedures, and regulations.

All of these will require various budgets to guide and control the carrying out of plans. They will also require a serious estimate of the understanding and attitudes of the workforce—management and labor—to gain some appreciation of how committed they will feel to the plans. Naturally top managers must approve plans and set them into action. However, if they have little understanding of people such as we covered in past chapters, the plans may never get off the ground as they had hoped and expected.

A very succinct argument for planning was stated in Tennessee Williams' play *The Glass Menagerie* when Amanda Wingfield, the mother, says to her son Tom: "You are the only young man that I know of who ignores the fact that the future becomes the present, the present the past, and the past turns into everlasting regret if you don't plan for it."

Changing Plans

The result of asking questions such as we have just noted leads many companies to make basic changes in their operations. This is especially noticeable in some of the firms that jumped on the conglomerate band wagon in the 1960s for a variety of good and poor reasons.

In the late 1960s Boise Cascade Corporation, firmly entrenched in the paper and paper-related business, started to acquire firms dealing in real estate and recreational vehicles and utilities, among others. In 1972 the firm lost more than $170 million and acquired a debt of over half a billion dollars. The company looked itself over and started to get back into forest products; it sold off hundreds of millions worth of nonrelated firms, which in 1971 had provided almost half of the total revenues.

Boise Cascade, under different management, has plans to double itself in the business it knows best by 1983 and hopefully, in the words of its present chairman, to "become and remain one of the top return-on-equity performers in the industry." At this point it still has a way to go to reach the industry's median of 15 percent.

National Can Corporation faced a similar problem in looking ahead. Years ago it, too, rushed into diversification, as did many of the other can makers. One of the pricks into diversification, apart from the general conglomerate fever, was growing anti-litter laws and demands for returnable bottles. Recently National Can decided to concentrate on the business it knew best: container making. It sold off a pet food division and a food-processing one, even though both together brought in $150 million in sales. Stated its president: "We're clearing the decks. . . . We are investing only in businesses we know and where there is a reliable profitability." Now the firm is almost totally in packaging operations.

Planning Down Below

Managers at lower levels in a large organization—and even in small ones—rarely get the opportunity to participate in the planning activities undertaken by senior managers. They should be encouraged to contribute to strategic planning by advancing ideas and arguments so they will feel part of the plan. However, final decisions in this area are the prerogative of top management, which assembles all information and attitudes.

The planning work at department levels, therefore, does not involve the same series of questions which we have just discussed. Nevertheless, unless they are working for seniors who think planning and managing by numbers is the best policy, lower-level managers still have to participate in planning activities. They need to study changes in objectives and policies, work out their own order of priorities, and estimate the flow of materials and services which will pass through their departments. They will also have to be concerned with personnel, for as we pointed out earlier, any person who is in a position labeled management but does not have any say in who works for him is really not a manager. He may have responsibilities, but cannot be held accountable.

Lower-level managers will also be concerned with their department budgets. They will also need to have proper communication with the people working in the department. There is a vital need for all managers to be basically sold on changes taking place and the work to be done by them. If they see problems that go beyond their department, they hopefully can feel free to discuss these with their immediate superiors; if not, they may have some explaining to do later on. If there is a lack of freedom to communicate easily upstairs, especially when there are major changes underway, that builds one more bottleneck into the operations. It is easy to build a "we–they" attitude in an organization. It gets a lower-level manager off the hook, because he can always blame problems on "them" upstairs. It is, however, an unhealthy attitude and certainly not helpful in carrying out plans successfully.

PROBLEM SOLVING

Although the lower-level managers do not make final judgments about plans for any organization, they are nevertheless required to undertake problem solving and decision making in their own departments. Planning involves looking at problems and potential problems and finding solutions and then applying these.

First Find the Problem

Before we look at the decision-making process, we should put in a word of warning. The biggest difficulty in decision making often is knowing what the problem is and particularly being aware of the problem fairly early in its onset. If a firm has made a big inventory of items before it is aware that the market for the items is rapidly going downhill, then it has a known problem of just what to do with its stock of items. But, if the firm were able to have seen the downhill trend some time back, the disposal of the old stock would not be its problem. It would have done something else and made money on its new item rather than worrying about how to lose least on its old item.

This applies equally to a service-type of organization if it doesn't keep in tune with what's going on. For example, preparing a report can involve a great deal of time, and if the thinking about the subject matter in the report is changing for various reasons, the report preparers should at least have some inkling of it and decide whether or not they should react to the changes and, if so, how. Otherwise a beautiful report can be prepared, but its usage may be simply in paper recycling.

It is exactly this which Peter Drucker refers to when he talks of the innovative objective of any organization. The role of a senior manager, at least in part, should be that of a problem sniffer-outer rather than only that of a problem solver. A good problem creator can be worth a great deal to any organization. Once a problem is fairly clear, as we shall soon see, there are guidelines for solving it. However, in life, by the time problems are sharp and clear, the organization frequently has missed the boat. Thus people or techniques that give early warning signals are vitally important. Textbooks can offer you problems and ask you to solve them; unfortunately, life doesn't flag problems as easily as writers can describe them.

Decision Making

Decision making is an art and a science. It is art when it comes to the selection of the key problems; it is science when it comes to the use of modern techniques for help in arriving at solutions; it becomes art again in applying the solutions.

Before looking more closely at the idea of decision making in general, it is instructive to note what Chester Barnard said years ago about the topic in *The Functions of the Executive:*

> *The fine art of executive decision making consists of not deciding questions that are not now pertinent, in not deciding prematurely, in not making decisions which cannot be made effective, and in not making decisions that others should make. . . .* Not to decide questions that are not pertinent at the time is uncommon good sense, though to raise them may be uncommon perspicacity. Not to decide questions prematurely is to refuse commitment of attitude or the development of prejudice. Not to make decisions that cannot be made effective is to refrain from destroying authority. Not to make decisions that others should make is to preserve morale to develop competence, to fix responsibility and to preserve authority.*

Steps in Making Decisions

1. Be aware of what are problems and what are not problems at a point in time. This also means looking for problems that are not obvious.

*Cambridge, Mass.: Harvard University Press, 1938. Reprinted 1968, p. 194.

2. The problems at hand must be clearly defined. Their definition depends on the objectives of the firm as well as the firm's attitudes to organization.

3. Once a problem is clearly stated, it has to be carefully analyzed. Here is where technical help is vital.

4. Analysis leads to solutions. Each solution has consequences for the firm and the people in it, and all these facts must be assembled. Again scientific techniques are invaluable, but consequences must also be seen in light of their effect on people and their relations to each other.

5. From the various alternatives, one solution has to be selected as the right one for the time. This is partly a continuation of step 4. Each solution must be weighed carefully and judged against the others. Questions which come up are:

- Which solution disturbs the organization's or the department's setup least?
- Which alternative is cheapest in dollars as well as effort?
- Would a startling change be best at the present time?
- Is a slow, almost imperceptible change more desirable?
- What people and configurations of people are needed to carry out each plan, and what does each desired change mean in terms of present staff and setups? (Although these are vital questions, it does not mean that a solution that is poor in most other ways should be accepted merely because it avoids human problems.)

6. The final stage is implementing the decisions reached. This involves a timetable and people. The effectiveness of implementing the decision also depends on how it will be brought to the attention of all the people who need to know.

Talked about in this way, decisions sound like grandiose solutions arrived at after weeks of examination and pondering. Big planning decisions are often of this nature, but decision making in itself is a common activity. The steps to go through are the same, even if company policies may quickly determine the solution to be applied. Decisions that follow a regular pattern should be set down on paper so that they can be implemented quickly when the occasion arises.

Unfortunately, decision making has become a glamorous term—as has the word executive. Decision making is thought of in terms of Hamlet's "To be or not to be" soliloquy. Normal decision making is a regular part of business, and if you can't make regular decisions without turning each into a major drama, then try another job.

Barriers to Decision Making

Decision making is a rational process. Douglas McGregor pointed out, as we have already noted, that man is actually a rational animal if we expect that this must also include coming to terms with his emotional side. A manager must understand this when involving those who work for him on the activities to be undertaken. He must also remember that his own emotional side is involved and that his own perceptions of the situation may not correspond with those of others. This can place a real barrier to successful decision making. It can show up in a number of ways:

- Too much evaluation and too little investigation.
- Arriving too quickly at simple solutions, which turn out to be superficial. Often a simple solution is the best one, but it should be looked at carefully and understood before putting it into effect.
- Failure to appreciate that new developments or experiences are not simply extensions of older ones.
- Failure to see the difference between problems and symptoms. If workers are spending too much time in the washrooms, does placing a TV monitor there solve the problem?
- Refusing to think deeply about problems which appear unsolvable because you cannot attach numbers to them.

With respect to the last item, people who are inclined to mathematics or simply scientific thinking often ignore things that cannot be quantified. By doing so, they leave out many elements of problems and arrive at neat solutions that do not solve the real problems.

The Brainstorming Approach

Sometimes a freewheeling approach to a decision to be made or to a problem in general can be useful. Such an approach should not take the place of other methods but should be in addition to them. The approach is particularly useful when no results appear to be forthcoming.

The best way to use the approach, which often goes under the name of brainstorming, is with a small group of people. Once you get to a dozen or more, the technique is difficult to use well. The objective of the exercise is to get everybody to suggest the ideas that come to his mind, no matter how silly or stupid they may sound. No one is allowed to criticize any suggestion. All suggestions are written down. A blackboard would be useful, as would flip charts. A secretary who takes shorthand would also help. As soon as an idea comes up, it is written down. People may build on each other's ideas but cannot disparage them in any way.

Such a session will probably not last much more than 15 minutes, although it could go on longer, depending on the problem posed and the people in the group. It shouldn't be dragged on too much after ideas start to die down. At that point—sometimes later on—all the suggestions are looked over seriously. Most will be immediately discarded. Some will trigger other ideas. At the end of the analysis there are usually one or two ideas which have merit and which would probably never have come out into the open if there hadn't been a freewheeling session with no holds barred.

Try it sometimes when no one is coming up with good ideas.

Critical Paths

A very useful planning system that can be used at various levels in an organization is the critical path method (CPM). A slightly more sophisticated version using essentially the same process is the program evaluation and review technique (PERT). CPM is often considered a primary stage in PERT. When these techniques are tied in with cost budgets for the activities involved, they can lead to major savings in money. CPM and PERT are useful when there is a series of events which are interconnected and lead to some final event. This can be an irregular activity such as scheduling downtime in an operation in order to do required maintenance, or it can involve a repeatable cycle of events.

Figure 5 shows an example. We start with an event we shall call A. This is a decision to go ahead with a project. A leads to activities such as assembling men and materials, a process that is completed at event B. In our example we estimate that this will take ten days, and we place that number on the line; an arrow is also added to show the direction of activities. B leads to the carrying out of four major activities: one leads to event C, a second to event D, a third to E, and the last to G. We draw arrows to represent the directions, and add in the estimated times.

Little can take place at C until an activity initiated at D is also completed. The B to C activity might, for example, require a foundation to be dug and the one from D to C require some scaffolding to be erected so that activity C to G (which may be laying down concrete and starting walls) can begin. Event D also starts an activity that has to be finished before E is completed. In similar fashion D leads to F, E and F lead to H, and F also starts an activity required to complete G as well as I, the terminal event. However, I is not complete until activities started with events G and H are also completed.

This is a relatively simple diagram showing the interconnection of a small number of events. Tracing our way to the final event I, we see that the longest path to reach it is A–B–C–G–I; if our numbers indicate days, then this path would take 60 days. Path A–B–E–H–I requires only 33 days. Other paths range from 30 to 55 days. The longest path in such a diagram represents the critical path.

Looking at the chart in Figure 5, we can see that there are some problems. If we go through all the paths using the times indi-

Figure 5. A critical path diagram.

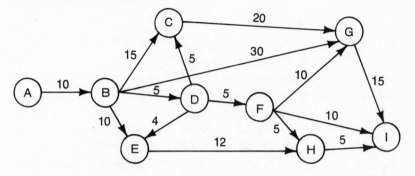

cated, then we will have completed some tasks days before others are completed. For example, if we go from A to B to D to C our time is 20 days. When we go from A to B to C our time is 25 days, yet we can't go from C to G before C is completed. We will therefore have five days' work open for some workers. We can either slow down the activity from B to D and D to C in order to arrive there in 25 days by using fewer workers, or we can speed up motion from B to C by increasing costs, perhaps by getting new machinery. Et cetera. We thus have a built-in system for planning (and controlling) activities in advance all along the line in whatever way appears most cost effective.

We would probably build in some slack to allow for problems so that if something broke down somewhere, we still had an extra day or so to complete that part of the work before time became critical. If, in the beginning, we went all out on all fronts, it would probably cost much more and create a number of new management problems. The more sophisticated PERT builds in variances in time at the beginning.

Both techniques are useful for a variety of operations. They require much work at the start, but good planning generally does. Once worked out for major projects, they can be computerized and manpower leveling carried out and adjustments made, when required, from time to time. Even on less than major projects, the thinking behind them is very helpful.

TIME MANAGEMENT

A very important aspect of planning is to ensure the proper use of that precious resource: time. This refers not only to deadline time for projects or parts of projects to be completed, but also to the regular, planned usage of time on a daily basis. Before we have a look at a variety of ideas that could prove useful, three points should be made.

First, if we examine the way we personally use time, we can probably agree that we all could make much better use of time than we do. We never seem to have enough time—but the fault usually lies with us and nobody else.

Second, different peoples have different conceptions of the use of time, and no simplistic set of rules can serve them all. Our personal approach to time is to a great extent culturally determined, and the "go-go-go" attitude that is supposedly characteristic of Western countries is not necessarily the way other peoples approach the use of time.

The proper usage of time is revealed by satisfaction and accomplishment obtained by the individual and the organization and not by early onset of heart attack, high blood pressure, or ulcers. Even in the West, there are many approaches to good use of time, and the computer-style approach is not necessarily the best one. Forced on people who can't work in simplistic linear fashion, it can lead to less being done than should be. Managers should be knowledgeable about the use of time by people who work for them and suit their allotted tasks to individual approaches as much as possible. Trying to remake people using the same cookie cutter may sound good but rarely works in the long run.

Third, the mechanistic view just mentioned is a popular feature of many books and seminars being promoted. It should be taken with many grains of salt. These writers and lecturers basically use a time-and-motion study approach to the work of managers, for whom the technique is least suitable. A manager is not handling machinery, at least not mainly, but people. He can use the basic concepts of a time-and-motion study approach if he keeps in mind that he is not supposed to be a robot. Some of the specialists go to great lengths with their advice, such as suggesting that people on the telephone not ask the other person how he is, as this wastes time. Another suggestion is that there should be no extra chairs in a person's office so that all those coming in must stand and deliver and thus do so more quickly than if they sat down. These are the types of people who would advise concentrated food pills for meals and short pornographic novels instead of sex.

Some Basic Ideas That Can Be Useful

Bearing in mind these three points, let us look at some of the basic ideas for improving our usage of time.

1. *Think of time as a resource to make use of.* This is a philosophical concept, but an important one. If you can think in these terms, you'll be better able to use time the way you already use other scarce resources.

2. Examine your activities to see if you really need or wish to make a commitment to save time. If you just like to talk about it, it isn't going to work. Examine your major activities and see how much waste there is in carrying them out. What other things could you do if there were more time available?

There has to be a real commitment to make better use of time or it will suffer the fate of organizational plans without any real commitment to them on the part of its members. Some people may not wish to save time in order to do more for the organization; on the contrary. So a real commitment to save time comes with a real feeling for the organization and a desire to benefit it because it benefits us. Senior managers often have great difficulty in understanding why more junior people do not have the same sense of loyalty to the organization as they have. They project their own attitudes on the others and fail to provide the environment where such attitudes could grow in their juniors.

3. *Set down on paper all your goals and objectives and list activities needed to achieve them.* This should be done with all of them, not just those you consider major ones. Some of the goals

will be major ones and could be listed as such. Others will be short-term ones—say six-month goals or so—which should be separated from the long-term ones.

4. *Evaluate the list of goals and establish priorities.* Mark those which have top priority, those which have medium priority, and those which have low priority. If you find this a bit difficult to do, first select the high ones and the low ones. Number the high ones and low ones in their order of priority, too, as this makes it easier to do. All the remaining ones are your intermediate-priority goals.

It is useful to recall here the point made by Peter Drucker to the effect that 90 percent of results typically are produced by 10 percent of activities and 90 percent of costs are incurred by the remaining resultless 90 percent of activities. Careful setting of priorities should go a long way toward reversing this undesirable picture.

5. *Make a daily list of things you have to do or are supposed to do during the day.* Write out the list at the same time each day, either before you start work or at night for the next day. Get started on the top-priority items and ignore all the others. As you check and revise your major list of items, the intermediates will tend to be upgraded to highs or downgraded to lows. They can thus be ignored with the lows until they become upgraded. If a senior person requests you to carry out what you consider a low-priority item, then it probably gets upgraded to a high one on the spot.

A word of advice in making your selections. Urgent tasks can often be taken for important tasks; they have to be done. Often, however, they are done at the expense of really important tasks. This is what is known as fire fighting, and if it occurs too often, it shows that you may need much more help than figuring out a better way to use your time.

6. *Keep a log for a week or two of how you spend your time.* You may be able to do so from memory. The purpose is to try to figure out which activities are your major time wasters. You'll probably discover these items on your list:

Reading and rereading paper.
Attending to minor matters.
Attending meetings.
General office paperwork.
Visitors and phone calls.
Waiting for replies from other people.
Attending to special requests from seniors or subordinates.

Looking at your list, you will probably find that there are some items over which you have little or no control, such as waiting for replies from other people and attending to special requests from your boss or even your subordinates. Without making yourself into an automaton, you may see ways to cut some of the time waste areas. In the case of meetings, it may be possible to have time limits set on some or see that better preparation is done on others, especially if you have some responsibilities in them. Poor preparation is usually the worst time waster in meetings. Well-prepared meetings take less time and generally lead to fewer meetings, since extra meetings are often just extensions of a previous one which wasn't prepared for. Similarly, in the case of minor matters that take up too much of your time, you might set yourself a personal time limit for making your decision. More often than not, lack of decisiveness is the reason for wasting time in this area. Remember Peter Drucker's 90 percent–10 percent rule!

Minor mail pieces and memos and notes, if not of obvious use, should be read and thrown away or filed by someone else if they contain information that may have to be consulted later on. How often have you skimmed through a promotion piece and kept it because you think it may mean something some time later? Forget it. Get in the good habit of throwing such pieces away. They rarely are needed later, and you will probably throw them away later because they are getting old—but after you have looked through them several times. This practice may help you make minor decisions relatively quickly and live with them even if some of them prove poor decisions later on. If you are perfect, you'll have a hard time being a manager.

Questions for Review

1. Write down the eight areas suggested by Peter Drucker for setting goals or objectives and give your opinion of each one in brief.

_____

_____

_____

_____

2. How would you apply some of these areas in a public-sector or social organization? Which would you delete? What might you add?

_____

_____

_____

_____

3. Discuss the boundaries or parameters of an organization and give examples (negative or positive) from your knowledge and experience.

_____

_____

_____

_____

4. Find out if your own organization has written objectives that are available. From your own position, do they appear to fit the reality?

_____

_____

5(a). Take any organization which you know about and comment on it in the light of the set of questions to ask in planning.

or

5(b). Create a small new organization to do some particular tasks and spell out a plan for it in the light of the list of questions to ask in planning.

_____

_____

_____

_____

6. Name some of the main barriers to decision making and give examples.

_____

_____

_____

_____

7. Keep a record of your own use of time over a one-week period, then analyze how that week was spent. What were the main time wasters during that period?

_____

_____

_____

8. What do you think could be done to improve your use of time?

_____

_____

_____

_____

_____

Case Study
The Jenkins Brothers

Charles Jenkins is a fairly new real estate agent but not a young man. He had been in various sales jobs previously and then decided to get into real estate. He has done reasonably well, and his manager, Oscar Peters, is quite satisfied with him, even though Peters is not the most approachable person.

One day Jenkins came to see Peters. "My brother," said Jenkins, "is a partner in the legal firm of Rogers, Hammerstone, and Jenkins. You may know of them." Peters certainly did. They did a lot of real estate work, although his firm had never had any dealings with them.

"I've certainly heard of them," replied Peters. "We have never had any work from them or used them. Are they interested in working with us?"

"Well," replied Jenkins, "yes and no."

"What do you mean?"

Jenkins let out a sigh and sat down. "You know the house on Buzzard Boulevard which John Strong here has listed?"

"Of course I do." answered Peters. "It's a nice house for $125,000."

"The son of old Rogers in my brother's firm has seen the house and likes it. He and his wife want to buy it."

"Good. Are you working on the sale?"

"There is a little catch. Cyrus Rogers wants to make a deal with the vendors, and he doesn't want to pay more than a $3,500 commission."

Peters looked at Jenkins for a moment. "And your brother suggests that we deal that way so the young man saves $4,000?" This would not be an illegal act, as commission rates were not set by law or even an association in the area where the firm operated.

"The suggestion is," said Jenkins, "that the former Rogers home, which will go up for sale, be listed with us and that the $4,000 saving can be worked out in various ways."

"Does your brother also suggest that we may get more business through his firm?"

"I can't answer for Edward," replied Charles Jenkins. "We are brothers and have been pretty close. So it is a good possibility."

Guide Questions

What should Oscar Peters do? What facts should he take into consideration in making his decision?

Case Study
Eclipse Machinery & Electronics, Inc.

Read over this case, which was discussed in Chapter 1, and draw up a three-year plan for it, making what changes you think are necessary and explaining why you are planning the way you are.

CHAPTER 4

Organization—the Means to Carry Out Objectives

Objectives are the starting point for organizations; they are obviously not the end point. Clear objectives are like a good start for a runner; they do not guarantee that he will win the race. There is much more to managing an organization than the possession of clear and proper objectives, essential as they are as a starting place.

One can hardly consider objectives without planning how to carry out these objectives. In practice these two often go hand in hand, so they are seen as intertwined. In essence, however, they are separate. First, the parameters and direction of an organization are determined, and in this process there is practical consciousness of the planning necessary to achieving the objectives. There must exist means whereby they can be achieved, or impossible objectives can be set. It is fine to have challenging objectives; it is ridiculous to have ones that are completely impossible to achieve.

Plans require a structure to carry them out, and thus a network of jobs and activities is created. What network is created depends on the needs of the organization. Different types of jobs have to be set up and the relationships between these—upward and downward as well as sideways—must be spelled out. What are the objectives of each part of the total organization, and how does each part mesh with the others to attain the objectives? Spelling out these facts is necessary for the smooth functioning of the total.

In brief, we can state that in setting up an organization, we must obtain the necessary resources, human and material, and so order and integrate them that people in the organization can carry out their assigned tasks and achieve the desired outputs. This must be accomplished within deadlines set for the work and within financial budgets, and it must produce the desired quality in the outputs and follow the methods and procedures set out by the policies of the organization.

Clearly, then, an organization cannot be a thrown-together mixture of various levels of managers and workers; it has to be a well-designed, logical system of relationships if work is to be performed efficiently.

THE ACCOUNTABILITY SYSTEM

The only type of system that could logically do what is required is an accountability system. Somewhere all along the line, people are not only responsible for getting the work done, whatever it is, but are accountable for doing so. Right up to the top, they accept the praise or the blame for what goes on beneath them. However, the accountability system is not automatic. It may have all types of logical parts built into it, but the judgments which essentially operate the system are human ones. Systems—mechanical, electronic, or mental—are guides, not gods. The critical judgments are human ones.

A work organization, then, is an accountability system that is based on human judgment. Judgment must be exercised at all levels in the structure, requiring that enough leeway be built into the system to allow for individual differences and human creativity, otherwise all everybody does is push buttons without thinking.

ORGANIZATION CHARTS

The formal structure is not simply an organization chart showing who reports to whom and what the main duties of each person are. Such charts are important and helpful in visualizing and working out relationships, but they are, at best, only a map of the living three-dimensional structure (actually four-dimensional would be a better description, for there are changes in time). A map of an area shows the relationship of one part of the area to another. It indicates rivers and lakes or oceans and their depths at various points and shows contours of the land and heights at various points. But the map is not the area itself. It is a flat representation of a colorful, rich and vibrant place on earth. But no one will deny that a map has important uses. The same holds true of organization charts and position manuals.

If you are a one-man organization, then you don't need a structure; you are it. It is only when an organization grows that it is necessary to divide up the work and decide who does what. And this is where all the trouble starts. How do you divide up work? Who shall be in charge of what? What will their relationships be to each other? And so on.

When an organization is still small these problems are just as important as they are in larger ones. They are not as complex, however, because fewer people are involved, and these people are generally in regular contact, so they can smooth out problems on the run. But a haphazard approach is no more justified in a small firm than it is in a large one. Why spend all the time smoothing out problems which needn't have arisen in the first place?

In the business world, the division of the work will depend on the type of business involved as well as the size of the enterprise.

A small plant will need a production side and a sales side. The importance of each will depend on the type of firm. It will naturally have to keep records, too. It may also have to have territorial groupings, depending on where and how sales are made. Often unstated, but highly critical, is the fact that someone has to decide first of all what market is to be served with what products and/or services and then keep a sharp eye on how the selected market is changing.

Special sections or divisions might be set up to service special types of customers or for the complementary product lines. No doubt there will be mixing of departments as well. A special-product-line division would itself be divided into finance, production, and sales and possibly other divisions. All will depend on the size of the firm and the nature of its products or service. A small firm could hardly organize itself into special product divisions, with each of these being further subdivided into finance, production, and so forth. It would be impractical to do this.

In many cases, managers will be salesmen or factory operators, too. When they are selling or operating, they are not managers. They have to combine the management work with the other jobs to be done in putting out a product or service or selling it. When the firm grows big enough, these men will find that they can no longer continue to successfully wear several hats, but will have to settle for the manager's hat. However, there are thousands of firms where the head person still must wear several hats in order to keep the company profitable.

In the non-business world, the divisions set up will have different names, but the pattern is similar. The structure required to properly carry out the work is created. Various aspects of the work are divided according to the needs and knowledge of the organization and its manager(s). In order to possess proper co-ordination of all jobs, each bit of a job must be properly shared out and a pattern of communication set up so that the best overall job is performed.

A one-man organization has no worry about job assignments or proper communication; these are all done by the one person. How to preserve as much of this oneness is the concern of the larger organization; as more managers are needed, the achievement of oneness becomes more and more complex and difficult. There must be communication, not only up and down, but also across departmental and other boundaries, or there will be hardening of the organization's arteries. Incidentally, these cross communications are difficult to show on an organizational chart. If they were all drawn in, the chart would look like the bottom of a hand-wired radio set.

BASIC BUILDING BLOCKS OF AN ORGANIZATION STRUCTURE

So far we were concerned with a general description of the organization structure and the communications within it. Can we say anything about the basic building blocks of the structure? What are its properties, or has it no real ones? How does it differ for different types of work and with time?

The basic building blocks in an organization are roles and role relationships. These words, like the word "work" itself, are used very loosely and in many contexts. For example, if somebody asked you what kind of work you did, you might reply, "I am a clerk" or "I am an electrical engineer" or "I am a salesman," or whatever. If a manager asked you, "How is the work going?" he is not referring to the same thing, but interested in knowing how much is being produced, whether it is on time and of the right quality, and so on. Again, if you were explaining some aspect of your work, you might say, "It is very difficult work" or "The work is not that difficult" or something of that nature.

We adjust to these various uses of the word work without even being aware of the differences between them. In the first case it is being used in the sense of the *role* being carried on in the workplace. This role concept also is important in discussing different positions of players in team sports. A center in hockey has a specific role to play. He may at times block a goal from being scored, but he is not a goalie. The same is true for other positions on a hockey team. Each man has a role to play, and in carrying out these roles, the team is doing what we call team work. The same situation exists in most team sports.

The roles of the team players are intermeshed to carry out their team objectives—to score goals or to prevent goals being scored, to hit runs or to prevent the hits from succeeding in obtaining runs.

As we all know, a problem with many sport teams is that, although they have capable players in various positions, they are not coordinated enough to become a winning team.

The same is true in the work place. The interrelationships of the roles are critical. In fact, the roles are meaningless unless they are interrelated with others to accomplish objectives.

In a real sense, an organization is like a mesh, where the nodes are the roles. The behavior of any individual in the organization is circumscribed in order that the interrelationships can be carried on properly and the work of the organization performed as required. Within the boundaries set for the role of the individual, there should be as much leeway as possible to give room to individual differences and initiative.

There are other boundaries of which we are not always aware, including legal ones and ones dictated by our own cultural background or individual upbringing. Often these are not properly taken into account by those who design and change organizations. The legal ones may be clear, even though there are problems with companies that have operations in several countries where the laws differ—and the social mores, as we have learned in some business bribery charges. The cultural boundaries are frequently assumed in English-speaking Western society to be basically British white ones, with the assumption that these are either common to most others or, if not common, desired by most others. Today this is not a correct assumption.

Four Organizations in One

The result of failure to take into consideration the information we have just covered is that we often generate what might be called four different organizations in one: the organization as it was designed to operate, the organization as it is seen to operate, the organization as it actually operates, and the organization as it should operate. There are problems in setting up, as well as changing, organizations. That is one of the reasons we spent the first half of this book on the human aspects. It is vitally important to have some understanding of people and why they behave as they do before looking at the structures in which most of us work. People have an effect on the organizations in which they work. At the same time, of course, organizations have an effect on people who work in them. Thus a case could be made for considering the organization first and then looking at the human side. Our view is that it is better to make the choice that we did. This is an interesting point and one which is very common in organizations where choices have to be made. There usually is something lost in going one way, and someone has to make the decision that the loss is less one way than going the other way.

Individual behavior in any organization, at any point, is the result of a number of factors, such as:

- The different personalities of the various individuals.
- The perceptions people have of each other.
- People's attitudes toward the constraints imposed on their behavior by their role relationships.
- The personal satisfactions or lack of them in doing the required tasks.

All these factors must be taken into account when setting up the organization structure. Also, as we already have mentioned a number of times, people's ethical and social constraints must be considered in order to avoid basic conflicts between roles played in an organization and those played outside the organization as husband, churchgoer, politically interested individual, and so on.

BASIC TYPES OF RELATIONSHIPS

There are three basic types of relationships which make up the mesh of structure, although even these are often mixed up in one individual.

The first is a straight boss–subordinate relationship. One individual, a boss or manager, is accountable for the operation of his section, department, or unit. To be a real manager, he has to have certain minimum rights and responsibilities. We touched on these before, but they bear repeating here:

1. The right to hire or veto new employees.
2. The right to decide what work is to be done by his subordinates.
3. The right to judge the performance of subordinates and award or punish them.
4. The right to move a subordinate out of his department or division.

Naturally, all this is carried on within the objectives, policies, rules, and regulations of the organization, and subordinates should have the right to appeal the manager's decisions. All four rights should exist at each management level, or there will be no real accountability of managers.

Understanding this is critical to setting up a structure, otherwise we could build all sorts of levels in a structure which wouldn't have real manager–subordinate relationships and without such relationships there can be no accountability system and no effective operation. We will discuss this question of levels of structure more thoroughly a little later on.

The manager in the situation we have just described has authority over his subordinates. As our definition shows, he has and exercises this power by virtue of the role he occupies in the organization. It is institutionally sanctioned power.

A second type of relationship is one where the question of the authority of one person over another is not that clear and sharp. This can occur in several forms. One is where a person is not working directly for another person—that is, for a particular manager—but offers him advice. This is referred to as a *staff relationship,* in contrast to the first basic type we mentioned, which is called a *line relationship.*

An engineering service person can advise a manager of a

department on the state of his equipment and tell him what needs be done. It is advice, and the department manager can take it or leave it, theoretically. If he ignores the advice and his equipment breaks down, then that manager can be in hot water. But the service man can't demand that the work be carried out or the manager will be fired. Neither can the department manager fire the adviser. Thus a critical aspect of the manager–subordinate relationship is missing. Other aspects, such as the right to punish and reward the other person, are inapplicable. The service man, of course, does have his own line manager, who has or should have the power to reward and punish the service man.

Another form of this advisory or service-type of relationship is when a manager has several supervisors (or whatever they might be called) keeping tabs on work. These people may alert workers when output is slowing down or quality is getting low, in which case the workers had better do something about the situation. However, they really have no authority to make the workers act differently, save that of their personalities. They assist their manager in doing things, but if you asked the workers who their real boss was, they would have little hesitation in naming the real manager. In the army, a sergeant orders men around, but the real boss of the unit is the lieutenant. Unless we recognize this, we get a chart that shows three levels when there are really only two (see Figure 6).

The third type of relationship is where there is no authority relationship at all, at least at that level. Managers of equal status in two departments in an organization do not have authority over each other. They may or may not have a common boss. Somewhere above there will be a common boss. In many organizations, managers have to cooperate with each other in order to properly process the product or services of the organization. Thus an effective relationship without authority has to be worked out and maintained. The greater the integration of the activities, the greater the need for effective relationships. Under certain conditions, such as where there are branch managers of retail stores in different locations, there is probably no need at all for any effective relationship.

Figure 6. A two-level, three-level department (a) as it is often set up; (b) as it should be set up.

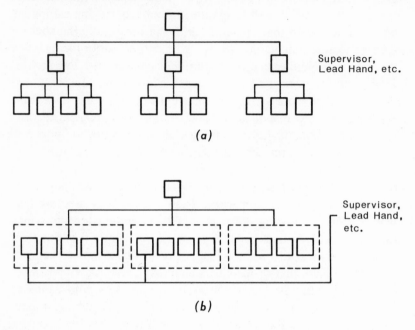

(a)

(b)

DELEGATION

Pursuing the investigation of the first two types of relationships takes us into an examination of the vital subject of delegation, a critical aspect of the work of any manager. We therefore are led to repeat in a much more personalized way what has been said previously.

Delegation involves giving a person responsibility and authority to carry out certain specified tasks. Whenever a manager hires people to perform various jobs because he cannot do all of them himself, he can either (1) tell people exactly what to do and keep on looking over their shoulders to see that they do it correctly all the time, or (2) tell people exactly what to do and give them the responsibility to see that it is done, checking from time to time to see that all is well.

Of course, he can also not instruct people properly and keep running around in circles to straighten out the work being done. In this case he would soon fall apart with exhaustion. The same fate might await him if he followed option 1 above. As the number of workers grew, he would get busier and busier as well as get all the people working for him pretty rattled by his activities. Should the same attitude be carried on by his own superior and by his superior's superior (if any), then all managers of the firm would be checking on each other all the time and chaos would be the result.

Thus option 2 is the practical way to go. This means delegating certain tasks, either managerial ones or physical ones, to people employed and making them responsible and, therefore, realistically accountable for their share of the organization's work. This doesn't absolve the first manager of accountability, for that is one of his tasks: to be accountable for the work of all others beneath him in his department, division, or unit.

To delegate properly is one of the essences of good management. The first quality required to do so takes us back to planning, and this is clarity. You cannot delegate what you cannot define. When a task is clearly defined, then one has to see that the definition of duties is clearly understood and willingly accepted by the person assigned to it, and also that the person is capable of doing it. The more complex the task, the more time is required to see that it is being done properly.

If delegation is clearly and properly spelled out, then it is possible to have one person work for two or maybe more bosses. This is supposedly a no-no, but in practice, it can be feasible at times. There are many of these so-called "principles" in management theory, many of which are not valid.

SPAN OF CONTROL

Another concern is how many subordinates one manager can have. This is referred to as *span of control*. Textbooks tend to say from six to ten; practice shows from one to up to a hundred. It all depends on what is realistic in the situation. Building up a structure with unnecessary levels just makes for a cumbersome organization; on the other hand, overloading a manager creates an impossible situation over any length of time.

The first question to ask in deciding on a span of control is how many subordinates are required; the second is the nature and complexity of the relationship. If there is a great deal of time required to be spent between a manager and his subordinates, then obviously one person can't control too many subordinates and still be accountable. The role relationships should be clear, and then the number of subordinates can be estimated. Use of supervisory relationships might help in some circumstances. Where a manager is required to do much counseling, training, and appraising of subordinates, the number of subordinates should be limited. Also, it will vary from technology to technology. There is no one commandment to serve as rule of thumb. The number should *not* be determined by thinking that a small group would be better than a large one. The first line of thinking is to preserve a realistic accountability.

From what we have already discussed, it can be seen that there are some patterns that can be followed in creating an organization. We can now take a closer look at what we might term the properties of the structure. There is no need to create or change an organization by the dart board technique—that is, throwing darts at a piece of paper and creating boxes where the darts land. There are, however, different types of structure that are appropriate for different types of organizations, so let us look a little at them before going on with some basic properties of all organizations.

An organization system is dynamic in character; that is, it responds to the environment, modifies its own behavior, and learns from experience. Therefore, some degree of change is a natural part of the routine behavior of the organization. Yet organizations can and obviously do have different philosophies or approaches to the problem of change. Some organizations are characteristically leaders in innovation and commit many resources to staying ahead of the others. Most organizations are followers to some degree, though making a reasonable effort to keep in touch with new developments. A few others are characteristically laggards that are always the last to change and concentrate most of their resources into refinement of existing procedures.

Obviously, different climates and styles of leadership would prevail in the three types of organizations. Those with the leader philosophy would devote a great deal of time to gathering information and planning in order to anticipate the need for change, while the laggards would devote little time to planning and would change only in crisis. Therefore, the organization's philosophy toward change would strongly influence the role of the manager in the organization in terms of his leadership style and his allocation of priorities to the various managerial tasks.

T. Burns and G. M. Stalker researched several British firms that entered the electronics industry after having experience in other more stable industries.* The firms that were effective in dealing with rapid technological and organizational change were those which placed less emphasis on their management controls. The ineffective firm in this study relied more heavily upon controlling and depended upon mechanistic organizational structures, which had been characteristic of their former environments. The explanation of the differences in the two approaches lay mainly in the behavior and attitudes of top management. Technical competence rather than traditional authority appeared to be much more successful in working out problems and coping with change. Recognizing the inevitable intensification of specialization, this leadership style permitted and encouraged widespread communication and cooperation.

Both the internal operations and the relevant environment can affect the nature of the differentiation and integration present in an organization. For instance, various departments can have different goal orientations, different time orientations, different interpersonal orientations, and different degrees of formality of structure. Combinations of these differences between departments could be determined by the actual needs of the operations of the department and its relevant environment. The environment, which can differ by rates of change, degree of certainty, time span of feedback,

*The Management of Innovation, London: Tavistock Publications, 1961.

availability of alternative markets, etc., can also affect the nature of the differentiation in the organization. In turn, the type of differentiation can influence the type of integration in the organization. For instance, those organizations whose stable environment allows a structure of low differentiation are often coordinated and directed by rules. Organizations whose unstable environment requires a high degree of differentiation cannot be coordinated in the same way.

C. Perrow* and J. R. Thompson† have analyzed the relationship of the structure of the organization system to the demands of its relevant environment. Perrow, for example, has concluded that a stable environment allows an organization to operate with relatively stable, routine operations, concentrating on efficiency and centralized control. As the environment begins to become less stable, differentiation begins to occur. The organization becomes more decentralized and less routine in its operations as the concern shifts to adaptation rather than efficiency. Thompson examines differentiation in a different way by looking at the types of interdependence between departments. Pooled interdependence occurs where all the departments, such as branches of a bank, contribute to the organization but rarely interact with each other. This type of interdependence is appropriate where the environment is stable and noncomplex. When the environment becomes less stable and more complex, the organization may have to shift to a reciprocal type of interdependence, which requires a great deal of complex interaction between departments and consequent complexities of integration.

While the work of various researchers may differ in terminology and emphasis, the direction of their findings is very consistent. The job of the organization concerned with long-term survival is to adapt its structure and its operations to the demands of its technology and environment. Certain types of organizational structures are more appropriate for certain types of environments than others. An organization whose structure appears to be out of phase with its environment therefore has to shift to a new structure in order to

*Organizational Analysis, Belmont, Calif.: Wadsworth Publishing Co., 1970.
†Organizations in Action, New York: McGraw-Hill, 1967.

continue to be effective. Accomplishing this sort of shift is of course a prime purpose of management development.

The increasing presence of government in the business world can also lead to a restructuring of a business organization. In 1977 Union Gas Limited went through a major reorganization of its senior management structure in order to devote more resources to the regulatory aspects of its activities. The change was also more conducive to its expansion plans and to achieving a broader base of operations. Essentially, what the company did was bring together, in a basically self-contained unit, all those concerned directly with utility operations. This group of vice presidents report to the executive vice president. The rest of the senior managers concerned with other corporate activities, including the growing regulatory ones, report directly to the president.

BASIC TYPES OF OPERATIONAL ACTIVITIES

In building the structure of any organization, whether a business or otherwise, we are concerned with three basic types of operational activities. We looked at these briefly at the beginning of this chapter. How they are mixed and what importance is given to each will depend on what the objectives of the organization are.

The first area deals with the design and development of goods and services. Some operations may start well back with basic research activities; others may restrict themselves mostly to development activities. But at some point there is concern for creating the goods and services which are the product of the organization. In a government department, creation of rules and regulations, as well as basic research of the true problems in order to devise the best rules and regulations, would come under this heading. In some organizations—particularly in "me too" companies—this area would constitute only a small part of the operations.

The second area deals with the provision of goods and services. It takes over from the first area in actually manufacturing the products or services in the form in which they are to be used by the customers or clients, whatever or whoever these are. This is the biggest area of most organizations. In industry it would be the factories; in nursing it would be the work associated with actual dealing with patients; in government areas it could vary from dealing with unemployed people to processing taxation forms, issuing checks, and the like.

The third major type of operational activity is the selling of goods and services. In some firms this may involve a full marketing operation interested in discovering needs of potential customers and making goods and services to fit these needs. In many cases it may be mainly a selling drive to push products or services which appear to be in common and constant demand. The selling side of government activities sometimes seems more obscure, but it ranges from hard-sell advertising in order to obtain tourists to low-key spreading of information about everything from old-age pensions to tax laws. It often has a full marketing aspect, since government goods and services are supposedly geared to the needs and wants of people living in the jurisdiction of the government body.

Obviously these three areas do not operate independently. They have to interact in order for the organization to function properly. For example, no real marketing can take place unless the selling side is in close collaboration with the designing and developing side. All the individuals have roles to play and are part of some interconnections in the overall organization web or mesh.

The financial side is a critical part of most organizations. It has not been mentioned here, because it is not an operational activity. It is vital to planning and controlling the operational activities.

Questions for Review

1. What is the main purpose of a work organization? Under what conditions is this achieved? Illustrate with examples, not necessarily referring to actual organizations.

2. What is the nature of an accountability system? What differences do you see between an accountability system in a business or government department and a voluntary membership system such as a credit union or social club?

_____

_____

_____

3. What are the basic building blocks of an organization?

_____

_____

_____

4. What similarities do you see between a role played by an actor and the role of a manager? What dissimilarities do you see?

_____

_____

_____

5. What are the basic types of role relationships in an organization? Illustrate with examples.

_____

_____

_____

6. Explain when and how a manager delegates. Illustrate with examples of good and poor delegation.

_____

_____

_____

_____

7. What is meant by span of control? In practice, how can you determine the span of control for a manager?

_____

_____

_____

8. What are the three main types of operational activities in a work organization? Do these occur in equal amounts in all organizations? Explain with examples.

_____

_____

_____

Case Study
Zedline Company, Inc.

By the early 1970s the Zedline Company Inc. was about five times greater in size than it had been some 20 years previously, and it employed 475 people in all. Over that time organizational changes had been made by addition rather than by reorganization. The President, Tom Zedler, still had a variety of responsibilities. He had been sales manager some time back and still was active in that area. He loved selling, and everybody said that nobody could sell the firm's products like Tom. In addition, a large group of people with various responsibilities reported to him, as shown by the organization chart for the firm (see Figure 7).

The main products produced by the company were in the transportation field and included automobiles, trucks, buses, trains, and even tractors. Some of the items could be used independently for various purposes. About 40 percent of the business was in the industrial field; the balance was in the consumer field, sold through a variety of outlets from department stores to specialty shops in automotive and other equipment.

Several of the top people in the company had started back in the old days when it was founded by Tom Zedler, Senior, during World War II and had received its initial push from war demands. One of these individuals was Roger Timmins, the secretary treasurer; another was Fergus Schmidt, the legal advisor and general all-round administrator. These people were very proud of the growth of the company but not very concerned with organizational growth in any planned way. Because of this they were frequently at odds with a younger controller, who had been installed there at the insistence of the company's auditors a few years ago. This man, Oliver Rebold, had tried to install some financial controls but was unable to do so effectively because of Schmidt and Timmins. Recently he gave himself one more year to do something; if he didn't succeed in that time, he thought, he had better pack up before he got too old to join another firm and move up the management ladder.

Fortunately the production side of the company was in more

Figure 7. Organization chart for Zedline Company, Inc.

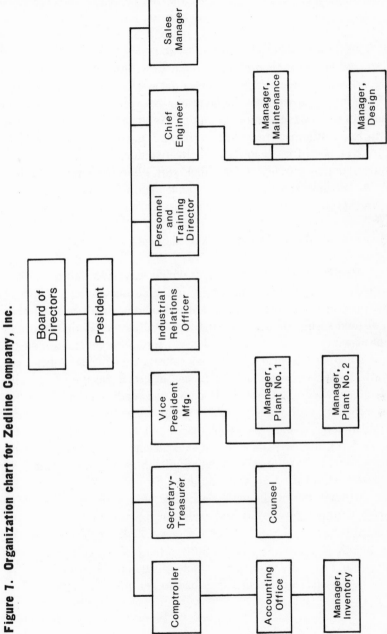

capable and more coordinated hands. Zedler relied very much on Oscar Remington, who was a very strong and experienced man in the manufacturing area and kept that part of the firm operating effectively. Still, there were a few basic problems even in this area. Production planning presented some difficulty, as did the design department, where making changes did not proceed smoothly. One of the problems was that the chief engineer reported to Tom Zedler and not to vice president Remington. Another facet of this problem was that Timmins, the treasurer, insisted on very rigid and uniform turnover rates for all items held in inventory. To maintain these rates required production runs that were often not large enough to be worthwhile from a cost standpoint. Tom Zedler had an "open door" policy and enjoyed talking to all who came in to see him. He always gave a sympathetic ear to the sales people even when they griped about Horton Barton, the man who had the title of sales manager.

Barton did have one problem which was never faced and corrected. His experience was totally in the consumer field. When he became sales manager, he wanted to do some work in the industrial field so he could learn what it was all about. Zedler told him not to worry, since he, Zedler, had all sorts of contacts in industry and some of the firm's industrial salesmen knew the ropes very well. The result was that Zedler was in effect the industrial sales manager, which he enjoyed. Because of spending his time on this and chatting with sales people, among other things, he had little time to look at the real problems of the firm and where it was headed. In fairness, it should be said that he was not really aware of impending trouble areas, and problems were rarely flagged so that they could be dealt with in advance.

Around the mid-seventies Zedler was looking forward to slowing down somewhat and becoming chairman of the board. Timmins retired. To obtain some money, Zedler sold some shares to outside interests, as did Timmins. This brought two new directors into the firm. The new directors studied the situation very thoroughly and decided that they had to get the firm to modernize. The two critical areas, they felt, were in marketing and the general organizational structure of the firm. They convinced the board that action had to be taken. The board agreed and even elected Leslie Parks, one of the new directors, to be the new president and to chair a committee to come forward quickly with a plan for reorganization.

Questions for Guidance

1. What ideas for investigation would you suggest to the committee?
2. What organizational changes would you suggest, and what is your rationale for suggesting them?
3. Draw up an organization chart for the new firm in line with your suggestions (see the old organization chart in Figure 7).

ORGANIZATION LEVELS AND MANAGERIAL QUALITIES

Organization, as we have seen, is concerned with utilizing and integrating the resources required to carry out the objectives of an organization. We have examined the roles and interrelations that are the building blocks of an organization, in particular, the basic types of relationships (direct line, staff or service, and cooperation without authority) and the minimal responsibilities essential for an operating manager. We have made the point, furthermore, that there is a type of system which is basic to effective organization, namely an accountability system, and we have examined the basic types of operations that constitute an organization. Finally, we have seen that organizational structures must vary with the technology used, with change in demands on the organization such as shifts in the market, and other factors. Thus we have examined patterns and building blocks, but we have not tried to construct any specific structures.

There is one major area which is rarely touched on in any logical way when discussing organization structure, even though it is highly critical. It is concerned with such questions as:

- How do you determine the ideal number of levels in a structure?
- What are the qualities required of managers at the different levels, and are they different?
- Are there optimum sizes for various organizational units as the organization grows in numbers? If so, when should levels of management be increased?

Some Basic Managerial Qualities

Research on the activities of managers at various levels has been done for many years. These studies show that at low levels, there is concern for the output of the plant or the office, for something specific and easily seen, in actuality or in the mind's eye. There is not too much broad planning activity going on. At senior levels supervisory activity is far less important and planning activity and the ability to think abstractly become much more so.

If we can sharpen up this type of investigation, then we should be able to look at the qualities of managers at low and high levels. It is obvious that a change takes place as we move up the ladder. A person who is capable of dealing with production problems and able to supervise people may not be able to think conceptually for more than a short span of time. Thus, whatever it is that makes for good management appears to be different at various levels. There is an apparent break between levels in the qualities required. There is a discontinuity, and this shows up in reality.

Every person can improve on a management job by study and practice, but it is probable that many people cannot move up to the top ranks merely by studying about it. We often say of an actor that he did a good job in playing Hamlet, or whatever role it was, but that he really wasn't big enough for the role. We say the same thing in practice about managers when we state that a person is doing a good job in his middle manager's position but isn't really big enough to move up to be, say, a vice president or deputy minister.

Some people may be middle-management or senior-management deaf. It isn't a matter of being a lesser person; it is a matter of not having the management capacity for the type of work involved. Until we get used to not being reverential to people of high position, we will have difficulty in dissociating position from personal worth. We managed to do much of this as our Western society moved from a feudal state with knights and barons and lords. We now tend to accept holders of power much more as people than our ancestors did years ago. Senior managers are moving into this popular mode of thinking, and although they still wield power over many people, it is not as absolute now as it was in the early days of capitalism.

Performance on the job in the beginning years of a person starting out in organizational work will probably show how far a person is capable of moving up the ladder, if proper and honest records are kept. These records will give indications of what we have called work capacity or management capacity. What this actually is, is hard for us to tell. It no doubt involves a mixture of intelligence, knowledge, skills, intuition, and personality; probably none of these is sufficient by itself. Certainly a manager should have a fair amount of intelligence, but people with very high IQs—if that is an acceptable measure of intelligence—do not always make good managers. Also, we saw, in looking at management styles earlier on, that there are a variety of effective styles for various occasions.

In sum, the capacity to do a management job effectively appears to be a special, complex phenomenon that expresses itself differently at various organizational levels. Let us examine in more detail what is known about working at various levels.

Managing at Various Levels

At the lowest level, that is at the shop or office floor, we have people who relate to things. We could say that such a person is a "concrete" kind of individual who enjoys work where the task is easily seen and where his activities are pretty well spelled out or obvious. This individual may be making a product where the process is well-known, or dealing with another individual on a simple basis, such as selling routine hardware items in a store. These are down-to-earth, concrete nonmanagerial activities.

The next step up is also mostly at the concrete level, but requires a little more imagination. Such a person has a few decisions of his own to make in order to complete his work successfully. One of these could be deciding which individuals will do the concrete tasks that need to be performed as part of the operation. Another might be to decide about making some minor rearrangements of activities in the tasks for which he is responsible. Thus there is more uncertainty built into work at this level, for an individual occupying a role there not only has to be accountable for seeing that the specific tasks are properly carried out, but he must be sure that he has made the best specific assignments to members of his work crew or rearranged the activities in a manner that leads to production improvements.

The third level involves a good deal of the concrete but also some thinking about the situation and what is necessary to keep the operation going. It requires that the individual has some visual control of the operation and, within that limit, can plan and work out ideas. A person running a small factory of some 50–150 employees is a good example. He can see the product being made, actually see where his raw ingredients are and when stock of one or another item is running low. He can also see the shipping room and whether or not it is getting bogged down or hasn't enough work to do. He may not see this from where he sits, although some of these managers have tried to have an office above the plant floor with lots of glass walls so they can literally see everything. Most managers at this level wander about the various corners of the shop from time to time and see what is happening in every part of it. They know then what to do.

At the fourth level, the person moves into being a pattern observer. He has some model of the operation he is concerned with and can understand what is going on from information supplied to him in reports, memos, sales figures, and the like. He knows what the norms of the operation are, and when he sees a distortion in the pattern in some area, from information flowing in, he investigates that area to get things back into shape. This type of person does not have to see the metal on the floor, the machines breaking down, or the social-work case load building up file by file; he gets this information in abstract form. He is no longer bound to the concrete. He can also see gaps in an operation which are not noticed by the close-range scanner.

In practice, the jump of a person from the concrete stage to the first stage of abstraction, which is pattern understanding, is one of the toughest jumps to make. Many fail to do so, for they cannot bring themselves out of having to see what is happening. If their business or department grows big, they may work themselves to death trying to control it, but the task is rarely humanly possible. Growth pushes managers to using abstractions to manage, and some cannot do this; the jump to the fourth level spells death to many.

At the fifth level, more abstraction is required. But there is another ingredient necessary as well. This requires playing with the patterns to see whether new methods can work. Not many people change methods at a low level. The manager at this fifth level is looking at the whole setup of the organization and relating it to the changing outer world as well. He then directs the new concepts which he feels will make the organization more complete. In essence, he is theorizing about possibilities and investigating them— or having them investigated—to make decisions as to where the organization should be headed. He is far removed from the visual manager, who mainly reacts to the events.

We will not attempt to go higher. We can see that each level makes a distinct change in the qualities of people required to successfully operate an organization. The levels we are describing start with the shop floor or office and go up the management ladder, with the fifth level being the highest we have described.

Several points should be made here. The first is that the qualities we have described at the higher levels may also exist at lower levels in individuals. This is an indication that that particular individual may have the makings of a more senior manager. Also, due to politics and family relationships, a person may be moved into a level beyond his management capacity. If he is intelligent enough and times are very stable and the business or organization is very stable as well, he may stay in his position with good helpers. But he will contribute little to the organization and probably make problems for those who come after him. It would be far better for the organization if that certain individual never had the top position.

Family businesses sometimes solve this by placing a member out to pasture. The Rothschilds, when they were beginning to grow in the money business, had the task of assigning five sons to take over and build the firm. The family considered the first four sons to be very able men. One was sent to open a branch in London, a second in Paris, a third in Vienna, a fourth to be general manager in the hometown of Frankfurt. The fifth son wasn't highly regarded as an able money manager, so the family sent him to Naples. There there was little business to do, so no great harm could be done while the son could still live an interesting life. The family did establish branches in other main centers, such as Amsterdam, but not with the number-five boy. There they employed outsiders to manage their affairs.

If we follow the four models of managers outlined, each of which differs from the others, we can see how to give a strong foundation to an organization structure. We can even see qualities of managers showing up at lower levels, when the individuals are young, which indicates the possibilities of some individuals moving up the ladder successfully.

Time Tells

There is another quality which appears to distinguish people at the various levels. This involves a time factor. Much work has been carried out on this in many countries of the world, including a number of Soviet bloc countries. The original effort, which still continues, was started in Britain by the behavioral scientist Elliott Jaques and by Lord Brown, then owner of the Glacier Metal Company, which made ball bearings. Jaques and Brown began in 1948 to investigate what work was in practice at Glacier Metal and what was the meaning in reality of managerial work and management levels. Their work spread all over the world.

One of the many fascinating ideas which came out of it deals with an individual's longest time of discretion in performing a task before he is properly checked on. Jaques* and Brown called it *time span of discretion.* They found a relation between people capable of operating at different time spans and management levels.

When we discussed the nature of human work in Chapter 1, we noted that it consisted of two major aspects. The first involved the knowledge and skills required to perform the work (this can be learned). The second involved a quality of uncertainty concerning the use of individual discretion in carrying out any task (this cannot be taught—it appears to be an inherent part of every individual). Some people need to be assured quickly that all is going right with their work; others can keep at a task for long periods of time without worrying about these assurances. The time span of discretion is related to this psychological feeling of uncertainty. Any person at any level can be called on to do a job in which the time span is only a few minutes or a few days. The critical time span is the longest one at which an individual can work.

Time spans are measured in terms of days, weeks, months, and years. Each task performed has some time span associated with it, although this is often unstated. A worker assigned to any task knows very well that he has to finish it within a certain period of time—not when he feels like it. A marketing manager asked to prepare some new marketing plan may not be told specifically when it is due, but he is well aware that a first report is due, say, within six months, depending on the nature of the plan and the business. Time span of discretion offers a tool that is like a thermometer: it can measure a quantity which is useful for practical purposes. Time span of discretion appears to be a similar instrument, possibly the first of its kind in the social sciences, and its use reveals some fascinating information.

*The information on levels and numbers is adapted from Elliott Jaques, *A General Theory of Bureaucracy* (New York: Halsted Press, 1976).

To effectively manage people who work at the lowest, most concrete level, a person should be successful in doing tasks that give him a time span of anywhere from three months to one year. He can ably manage people whose own time span ranges from several days to two months or so. If he has a five-month time span himself, he will have trouble with a person working at a time span of three months. That man would look above for his real boss.

A manager operating at the next level can go from one to two years. Above that level a person has to break away from visual control to pattern observation, and there the time span of discretion is from two to five years. At the next level, and this is the fifth level of an organization, the time span goes from five to ten years. There are other levels above these, but these take us far enough along the trail.

There are other numbers attached to these time spans—in particular, those relating to the number of individuals who can be effectively managed at each level. These numbers are not absolute, but depend on how labor-intensive the organization is.

At the second level, the first real managerial one, the number of employees could go to about 50 people. If the number exceeds that in a labor-intensive outfit, then it is probably best to select another manager at the same level and divide the operation.

At the third level, the number of employees could go up to 350 people, even a bit more. (See Figure 8.) Here a manager with a good visual memory will be able to recognize all the people employed, and they will probably recognize each other as well, even if they do not know names. Beyond that number, anonymity sets in and it is better to again divide the group into smaller ones. Remember that we are dealing with top numbers here; in many cases, division should come earlier on.

The fourth level could encompass up to 2,500 people and the fifth one up to 20,000 employees.

INFORMAL GROUPS

In discussing organization, we have so far not mentioned a favorite distinction used by many writers in this field: the "formal" versus

Figure 8. Desired number of levels in an organization (full details not shown).

Three Levels

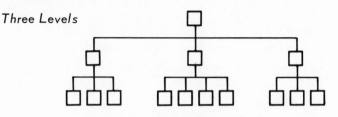

Time span of head: one to two years
Maximum number of employees: about 350

Five Levels

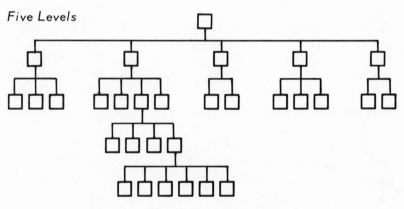

Time span of head: five to ten years
Maximum number of employees: about 20,000

the "informal" organization. The first supposedly corresponds to the rigidly drawn chart showing the organization as management hopes it is; the second comprises the subculture groupings that get set up inside the formal organization, because people are as they are. The informal organization can fight the formal one or work with it or passively and unenthusiastically go along. The idea originally emerged from the work of Elton Mayo and the Hawthorne experiments described in an earlier chapter.

There is no doubt that people group together inside organizations and that these groupings are important. Mayo pointed out that these subgroupings or informal groups arise because of a void not filled by the management structure. Actually, in all the work he did (which helps us greatly now) Mayo never made any analysis of the superstructure of roles that allocated work to people and set the policies within which the work was controlled. Mayo, in other words, never really examined the organizational setting in which the Hawthorne workers operated. He examined their attitudes and their feelings.

The idea of an "informal" and a "formal" organization living together stems from a basic misconception of the very nature of an organization. Earlier in this chapter we noted a number of role relationships. The first was the boss-subordinate relationship: many of these are strung together to create the operating spine of any organization, consisting of fully accountable managerial linkages. The others were a variety of support or staff roles and we spelled out a few of them. In reality there may exist as many as ten different support roles. Many observers think of the operating spine as the formal organization and fail to seriously examine the many support roles that are also part of a management system. The main reason this happens is undoubtedly the lack of precision in defining the support roles.

Informal groups will set up when the support roles are carelessly thought out and incorporated into a structure. The presence of them is a sign of managerial weakness—unless, of course, they are basically concerned with social and sport activities. When these support roles are carefully considered and utilized, they make an organization whole.

ORGANIZATIONAL CLIMATE

If we obtain a proper people style of organization, we should create what has come to be referred to as a good organizational climate. The term organizational climate has become common only over the last decade or so, although the ideas implicit in it go back many years. Some people have referred to it as the personality of the organization, but in actuality it probably goes beyond this idea. It is the perception by members of an organization of the attributes of their organization and the ease or unease with which they work in it. Thus the organizational climate can vary from individual to individual and from department to department.

Organizations may theoretically have as many climates as they have members, particularly if the members are drawn from many different cultures as well as a variety of upbringings. In practice there will be a much smaller range in most organizations, and undoubtedly lumpings of climates in various departments.

People's attitudes to their work are based on their perceptions of things. If there are means to investigate organizational climate, this should help in arranging desirable organizational changes in order to create better climates.

Some researchers in this area found that most of the managers they surveyed had a feeling of highest job satisfaction where there was an affiliation-type climate. Next highest was the achievement-type, and lowest was the power-type climate. However, other investigations revealed that managers and salesmen are more satisfied in an achievement-oriented climate than in an affiliation- or power-based one.

There is no full agreement on what dimensions to use to measure climate, and there are a variety in existence. The following six have been used in businesses and with employees ranging from sales types to plant supervisors. They are based on the work of Herbert H. Meyer in the General Electric Company.* They are:

Constraining conformity—the degree to which people feel that they are constrained by a multitude of rules, procedures, policies, and so on.

Responsibility—the feeling of people that they are given a lot of responsibilities and can do their work without having to check all the time with a manager or supervisor.

Standards—the emphasis that people feel is put on performing well, including the knowledge that challenging goals are always kept in mind and people feel pushed to achieve.

*Reprinted in *Organizational Climate: Explorations of a Concept,* R. Tagiuri and G. Litwin, eds. (Cambridge, Mass.: Harvard University Graduate School of Business Administration, Division of Research, 1968).

Reward—the degree to which people feel they obtain a fair reward and are not always jumped when something goes wrong.

Organizational clarity—the perception that things are in shape rather than chaotic, confused, and disorderly. This does not mean too tight a constraint, as in the first dimension.

Friendly team spirit—the existence of a general cooperative feeling, with managers and others trusting each other and people proud to identify with the firm.

Checking organization members on these six or other factors involves seeking their responses to certain statements which are used to show up the six (or more) dimensions. It is not a "how do you feel about . . . ?" type of survey aimed at indicating morale in an organization. The two are related, but the morale survey is much more personal than a climate survey.

A number of researchers, including Renato Tagiuri and George H. Litwin of Harvard,* have developed a series of questionnaires to show up the climate. Such a questionnaire might contain a statement such as: "The organization develops good ideas ahead of others." People are then asked to do two things separately. The first is to rate their ideal organization by giving it a low or high mark on that statement. A scale of 1 to 7 would do, with 1 indicating that this is hardly ever done and 7 indicating that this happens very often. The second thing to do is to use the same scale and rate what they perceive as the practice in their organization or department.

Other questions might be:

Experienced members take time to help new people.
There is a sense of purpose and direction evident.
There are clear "in" and "out" groups present.
People obtain most of their information about the organization from those outside it.

The analysis of the results would show us two things: (1) what people think is an ideal type of organization, and (2) how people rate their actual or perceived reality. The second item shows the organizational climate. The difference between the two ratings in-

*Ibid.

dicates whether or not there are problems present, and by assigning the answers to the dimensions used, it is possible to see where the problems lie. This is the first step to improving the climate and the organization.

Questions for Review

1. Describe basic differences which you have noted in managers at various levels in an organization from your previous readings and experiences.

_____

_____

_____

_____

2. What do you think managerial capacity is?

_____

_____

_____

3. Describe the five first levels of an organization as it should be and state the major differences between people performing at each level.

_____

_____

_____

_____

_____

4. Write down some of the main tasks you perform as part of your job now and figure out what your time span of discretion is for each.

Task	Time Span of Discretion
(1)_____	_____
(2)_____	_____
(3)_____	_____
(4)_____	_____
(5)_____	_____

5. What is your opinion about informal groups? Give some examples of which you are aware or which you have personally experienced.

_____

_____

_____

_____

_____

_____

6. Below are a number of statements which reveal aspects of organizational climate. First consider an ideal organization. Read the items and grade them on the left of the page. Use this for grading: _1_ means almost never; _2_ means infrequently; _3_ means sometimes; _4_ means often; _5_ means very often. When you have done this, go over the items again and, on the right-hand side, mark them as you think they apply to your organization as it operates now. The items are in two parts, and you obtain two totals on either side of the page when you add your marks.

Ideal		_Reality_
	PART ONE	
_____	The organization is ahead of others with new ideas.	_____
_____	It encourages people to use their own initiative.	_____
_____	Older workers are helpful and friendly to new people.	_____
_____	Managers are pleased to listen to new ideas from others and use them.	_____
_____	Managers consult members to see if they have usable ideas on assorted problems.	_____
_____	There is a good feeling that the organization is going somewhere.	_____
_____	The organization helps members acquire new information and skills which will help them perform better.	_____
_____	(Total)	(Total)	_____

DIFFERENCE BETWEEN THE TOTALS: _____

Ideal   *Reality*

PART TWO

_____ General conversation is always about problems.   _____

_____ There are definite "in" and "out" groups in the   _____
organization.

_____ Members always have grievances, no matter   _____
what is done.

_____ Members quit because they are not properly dealt   _____
with.

_____ Members learn more facts about their organiza-   _____
tion from outsiders than through internal communication channels.

_____ (Total)   (Total)   _____

DIFFERENCE BETWEEN THESE TOTALS: _____

SUM OF THE DIFFERENCES: _____

(Largest possible difference is 48)

Case Study
Worthwhile Employment Service

William Alexson is president and general manager of this firm, which employs close to 400 people in a major city. He is not the founder of the firm. This man is Partial McQueen, who is chairman of the board and chief executive officer but only comes around and interferes with operations from time to time. Alexson has been with the firm for some 15 years, having done almost every job in the operation during that time. He has been running the firm itself for some four years, ever since the time McQueen decided he wished to do other things and take off whenever he felt like it.

The firm is in the temporary employment service field. Its main supply of people is in the clerical, stenographic, and receptionist areas, but it also handles skilled trades in industry and commerce, such as draftsmen, technical assistants on engineering jobs, and so on. These latter jobs are handled through its commercial and industrial division. All other positions are filled through offices in 13 locations around the city and surrounding towns. Occasionally the branches handle a skilled tradesman request even though they should refer them to the special division. Head office says nothing about this.

The head office itself is rather small. Aside from William Alexson, there are a two-man accounting department, a one-man personnel department, and several people who do general office work, including secretarial work for Alexson and Brent Rentbers, the accountant.

The 13 general branches vary in size from about one dozen people to some 75 in the largest one. Turnover is high, and no office has ever been fully staffed for very long.

Despite the problems in the firm, business itself is fairly good. Alexson is mainly worried about two major problems. The first is the staff turnover, even at the branch management level. (A couple of the large branches have assistants to the managers.) The second problem facing Alexson—and this he thinks is his major priority, as high turnover is characteristic of the industry—is that he feels he has not got a tight enough grip on what is going on, except in a general way when he gets his weekly reports. He wishes to give his managers much leeway, and this applies as well to most of the individuals working in each office, but thinks that he requires more control and much more conscious planning ahead for the firm in general, and each branch in particular. He knows that he can't formulate plans without good help from his branch managers, and good plans are meaningless unless he can keep some control of what is happening about them.

Questions for Guidance

1. What would you do about this situation?
2. What information would you want to collect before you made basic changes?

CHAPTER 5

Staffing, Directing, and Controlling

We are combining the three functions of staffing, directing, and controlling in this chapter because they interrelate considerably. They are the means of keeping in operation the organizational structure which was built to be the vehicle for achieving the plans set to meet the objectives of the organization. These three functions might be compared to the motor and the driver of the vehicle. They are heavily dependent on understanding the material covered in Chapter 2—the human aspects. Although all the other functions require good practical knowledge of the human aspects, as we have seen, staffing, directing, and controlling make more open use of this knowledge and the skills associated with it.

Two items should be noted here, for they will not be covered specifically in the following material but only treated in a general way. The first one is union activities and relationships. They are part of the overall problem of communications and constitute parts of two boundaries of an organization: the legal one and the social and cultural one. We talked about these and other boundaries in discussing organizations. Where unions exist—and they do in most big organizations today—these legal and social-cultural boundaries add extra limitations on the operation of an organization.

The second item is concerned with change and specifically changing times. This is evident to most people but often not taken into consideration practically in managing organizations. It leads to an incorrect statement that younger people do not wish any structure at all and only favor anarchy and chaos. Some probably do, and there have been people like them for centuries. Most humans will accept structure and in fact desire structure, but it must be perceived as relevant to new times and not to old ones.

Members of the younger generation of the sixties who opted for anarchical communes with no essential planning, organizing, directing, and controlling soon found themselves in an impasse and went down the road to murder or shunted so far back that their members became more conservative than their parents. The older generation (at least those in positions of control) failed to see that new approaches were required to fit in with new social and cultural thinking. Many individuals were forced to fight the so-called establishment because they had no room to grow as people unless they chose to fight. It was a losing fight and hurtful to many. Possibly those in positions of power now will have to recognize that new approaches always are required and that the struggle for them need not be bloody and considered anti-organization. The scenery changes, the names change, roles change, but in essence, the organization endures forever.

STAFFING

Recruiting involves the selection of people to fill the various roles in an organization. The selection process is always a predictive one: we are predicting that the person employed will perform at least satisfactorily in the job to which he or she has been assigned.

For many jobs the selection process is quite simple. If the

work involved is relatively easy and takes only an ordinary amount of brain power, then almost anyone who applies can be hired. This is fine if the individual has little desire to grow and develop on the job; if he has and is thought of as general labor by the employers, he has to fight much harder to advance than if he had been hired into a higher-level job in the first place. The organization, as well as the individual, loses out. Many people are hired in this manner also for sales jobs, even though we are aware that a strong need for achievement should be present.

The technique for selection used in cases such as we have just noted is sometimes referred to as the PPG test. PPG refers to Pittsburgh Plate Glass: if the potential employee breathes on a piece of glass and it shows evidence of life in the body, that person is hired!

In hiring there are many, many techniques used and countless tests employed. Rather than knowing the details of these, a manager should know what the process is all about first. Techniques can then follow, suitable to the needs for the position—and, alas, often suitable to the ego and power desires of those doing the hiring, whether they're personnel people or the final manager.

The recruiting process requires first of all exact knowledge of the position for which we are hiring a person. We can then evaluate from our interviews and tests whether or not the candidate can perform well enough in the work. It is often lack of real knowledge of the position and the knowledge and skills it requires that constitutes the stumbling block.

All positions should be clearly identified in the organization with the relationships known to other employees. The first requirement would be to work out the level of the position in the manner we discussed in Chapter 4, where we dealt with the determination of the number of levels required in any organizational unit. Unfortunately, this is often not the case. In many organizations, jobs develop by chance, by personal political gaming, and by straight copying from other organizations. Before hiring it is useful, if the managers are willing, to take a new look at the position, particularly at higher levels.

If we have to select a person to fill the position, then we have to know enough about that position in order to tailor the selection process to the job requirements. We should also be aware of how much growth potential is permissible in the position.

Facts to Know about Positions

Here is what we should know about each position:

- The tasks that have to be performed.
- The general areas of competence required.
- The knowledge and skills obviously needed to demonstrate the competence.
- The knowledge and skills that would enhance the performance on the job but are not as obviously needed as those in the previous item.
- The time span of discretion that is usual for the job. This is more essential in higher positions than at the ground level but is still a factor that should be understood at all levels.

In many ways the best place to get some of this information is from people who are considered very competent on similar positions or their immediate managers who are well versed in the position.

What is available most often in hiring is a list of the tasks to be performed, a list of the personal requirements, education, and some skill knowledge, such as the ability to type at 75 words per minute with a minimum number of errors. It is a tribute to people that despite the crudeness of some of the selection processes used in organizations they perform well on the jobs. It is also, of course, a source of many problems for the individuals hired and for the organization afterward. In hiring people, one major factor, which stems directly from the ideas covered in Chapter 2 dealing with motivation, should be borne in mind: a person who understands his job and likes at least some of it will be much more highly motivated on the job than someone who has to learn much of his job while working on it and has little real liking for any of it. And a person who is already motivated is a much greater asset than an individual for whom we must figure out what to do to really motivate him. Obviously, this choice is not always easy to make, but it is a factor one should bear in mind in hiring.

We will not go into detail on forms used and testing methods, of which there is an endless variety. The forms used should provide for information such as we noted in the last paragraphs and some sort of evaluation of how the person being considered appears to fit. Some of this would come from answers concerning the knowledge and skills possessed by the potential recruit, but it is useful to write down some overall impression. This could be simply ticking a spot on a line marked completely unsuitable at one end and extremely promising at the other. Testing should be carried out by professionals and not by amateurs. The hiring, however, should be done by the organization in the final phase. Test results should be taken as one input to the situation and not as the deciding factor, particularly for more senior positions. If test results reinforce other inputs, good; if they don't, then the situation should be looked at again. If other factors still say no and tests say yes, or vice versa, the general advice is to forget the tests. Tests also should not be too long and exhaustive. A few hours should reveal as much as is required.

Sources of people for positions vary a great deal from straight advertising to soliciting letters and inside personnel. A firm that keeps up-to-date records of its employees should make use of this information when jobs become open or new ones are created. However, only honest and thorough records are suitable. Large organizations can do this on a computer, but such sophistication is not essential. When used this way, good records, aside from their own value, are helpful to general morale in that they enable the organization to follow a systematic policy of rewarding employees who have demonstrated some growth in skills and abilities. Internal promotions also provide already indoctrinated individuals, saving time and dollars.

The Employment Interview

One critical aspect of recruiting is the hiring interview. We will go into this in some detail, because it is generally poorly handled, not out of stupidity but due to a lack of understanding of what it is supposed to accomplish and what the problems are in carrying one out. This will take us into the broader subject of interviewing people—an important aspect of any manager's job. We will go into this subject in more detail later in this chapter. Here we will focus on the employment interview itself.

What actually is an employment interview? Or, for that matter, what is an interview? Is it a lecture? Is it a discussion? Is it a social conversation? Is it an interrogation?

It may in fact contain some aspects of each of these, but it is best defined as a face-to-face contact between two people with the goal of getting and giving information. It is a *conversation with a purpose*—in our case, to hire or not to hire an individual. The three basic steps in the employment interview are:

1. Establish friendly rapport.
2. Obtain required information.
3. Give required information.

The most common mistakes in employment interviewing are:

1. Doing third interview step before second.
2. Failing to prepare properly for the interview.
3. Failing to get the person interviewed to talk freely and give required information.
4. Failing to remain neutral.
5. Failing to ask direct and probing questions.
6. Failing to listen carefully and remain silent even if recruit appears at a loss for words.
7. Failing to control the interview.

The questions to be asked should be worked out in advance and should be in some logical order. They should also be open-ended. Instead of asking a person if they obtained good grades in school, inquire how they got along in school. The former makes the interviewee feel that he should answer that he did well or find some way of getting around the question if he didn't; the second form lets him answer more freely.

The basic idea of the interview is to obtain a picture of the individual and then make up your mind if he fits your requirements. If all the requirements are given first, he will tailor answers to those specifications. If the questions are not thought out and ordered, then the view obtained is confusing. The interviewer should talk little and let the potential recruit do most of it. If the recruit doesn't do about 70 percent of the talking, something is wrong.

Here are some things to watch for in evaluating an interviewee:

Appearance—need varies from job to job. A military look is not required, but easy contact with public and peers is a good guideline.

Manner—pleasant and as relaxed as possible in the situation and not suspicious and antagonistic.

Speech—varies from job to job, but a clear and easy way of expressing things is useful.

Training—formal and informal training to meet adequately the needs of the position.

Skills—possesses skills adequate for the position.

Work experience—useful for current position or not? Is growth shown in past position? If candidate held a variety of positions, has this led to maturity? Can he or she evaluate work on past jobs objectively?

Sociability—again, job determines need, but an uncooperative person may do more harm than good in a friendly work group.

Motivation—is there evidence of goals and interest in achieving them? Are they realistic ones?

Stability—related to work experience. If candidate is a flitter with no signs of growing maturity, he or she may flit off the new job quickly, too.

Perseverance—what is the evidence of ability to stay with a task? Do education and work history show lack of ability to stick with something?

Physical energy and drive—is person listless in approach and probably not willing to work hard (and overtime) when required?

Self-reliance—does recruit seem to be a leaner and will require constant management support?

Induction and Orientation

Once an employee has been hired, he is often neglected after that point, particularly at the middle and lower levels. Hiring at a senior level generally includes an induction type of program before the person is accepted or accepts the position. Neglect should never face an employee at any time in his career, but it is much more harmful to the organization and to the individual when the employee is starting on a new job.

There are at least two parts to any induction program, and they should be worked out in advance. The first is to provide knowledge about the organization and its people. Especially in a large firm, such an orientation program can be automated to a great extent. The second is gearing the individual into the work, and this should not be rushed but spread out over a period of time. Let's consider the contents of both.

The orientation program could include the following elements:

- A "welcome to our organization" leaflet or talk.
- Information on hours of work and break periods.
- Information about pay, salary progression, pension plans, sharing of medical costs, and so on.
- Eating and parking facilities.
- Vacations.
- Forms—if any—still to be completed and turned in by a new employee.
- Organization history, main activities, executives, and major divisions and departments.
- Introduction to peers and others with whom the new employee is likely to come into contact on a fairly regular basis.

Much of this can be accomplished with printed material, although there should be someone available to discuss the contents of the material as well as to show the new person around and make introductions, perhaps to ask him to lunch in the first day or two, even if this is just eating sandwiches in a lunch room.

The nature of the work to be done should have been made clear during the interview. The knowledge and skills possessed by the employee should also be known. The introduction to the practical side of the activities should be scheduled over a period of time and the person introduced to them on this planned basis. The employee's ability to cope with the new reality will be uncovered during this period. The organization will also discover what training is required to improve performance. It may well turn out that the best decision is to "de-hire" the recruit because he or she shows no evidence of being able to handle the tasks. If the organization is large enough, this may not mean firing but placing the individual in another position.

The planned introduction to the work should be spelled out on paper and comments made by various supervisors involved—if there is more than one—about progress in the time allotted to understanding the specific task(s) set for the period. This provides a written record of progress and the means to adequately judge performance over time. Keeping these items and comments merely in one's head rather than committing them to paper is the conceited or lazy person's way and rarely good enough.

Questions for Review

1. How do you interpret the changed attitude of many younger people to organizations and managers? Take into consideration such items as attitude to structure, new concerns for environmental factors, and lack of interest in concerns of previous generation. What, if anything, should today's organizations and managers do differently?

2. What facts should one know in recruiting?

_____

_____

_____

_____

3. What are the main steps to take in an employment interview, in proper order?

_____

_____

_____

4. What are main difficulties encountered in conducting employment interviews?

_____

_____

_____

_____

_____

5. Read the following information and write down the main questions you would prepare for in an interview with the candidate.

Wanted: Young man or woman to work in field of accounting in industry with good possibility of management position in the future. Should have university or community college training or equivalent and several years of experience.

Candidate: Wilbur Forkton

• Education: Completed high school in Kingston, Ontario. Went to a community college and studied commerce and accounting in a business program. Received certificate on completion of the program.

• Work experience: Worked in supermarket as bagger and general help, part-time during school and full-time in summers. After graduation from community college went to work for an insurance firm in the accounting section. Was asked to participate in sales training and promised more money if he became successful salesperson. Wasn't happy in this role and after trying some time left the company.

Worked in office of supermarket but after a year of this decided that there was little future unless he wished to become a manager of a store. Decided that this wasn't for him and thought that work in accounting area in a larger firm or plant might be better for him and offer him more opportunity, so he left the company.

• General information: Forkton was one of five children. Father was killed in a plant accident when Wilbur was nine years old. Worked part-time soon afterward to help family make ends meet. Not very active in sports except in tennis and prefers doubles games. Watches other sports on TV mainly, rarely going to a professional game. Dresses neatly, is of slim build, and clean-cut in appearance. Quiet in speech and tends to be somewhat nervous.

6. Suppose you have hired a person to fill the position outlined in the previous question. What steps would you then take with the new recruit?

DIRECTING

Before examining the areas of communication, evaluation, and appraisal, it would be useful to discuss two broad items that could come under directing in general. One is a well-known and often useful principle termed *management by exception;* the other is a popular approach generally going under the pompous title of *management by objectives,* or MBO.

Management by exception is based on a quality control concept. When certain specifications are called for in a part being produced, they are set up with certain tolerances. Any item that stays within the tolerance figures is accepted; those which do not are rejected. Using this principle, a manager can develop acceptable behavior by a variety of standards and not check into this behavior, at least not regularly, as long as it stays within the set boundaries. If, for example, production keeps on at an acceptable rate, the department manager may safely ignore this aspect of his job and instead turn to more pressing matters. Standards may also be set for people approving expenses up to a certain value as long as it is within budget. Above this value, the manager next up the line has to be consulted. Exceptions apply when things are going much better than expected as well.

This is a very acceptable principle; it allows free time for individuals to perform without being carefully watched all the time, and it permits the manager to go about his various duties without always watching what is going on. In many ways it is an adaptation of ideas which we discussed in the previous chapter. However, it has obtained a life of its own and is concerned with directing of staff. It should not, although it might, do away with a full appraisal, from time to time, of what is going on. An accountable manager would not permit this to happen. Thus, if it is regarded strictly as a gimmick, it can have harmful effects.

Management by objectives stems mainly from ideas first stressed by Peter Drucker in his book *Managing for Results*.* The name is rather pompous, as we have seen that all organizations should have objectives and their basic purpose is to meet those objectives. MBO has been actively used under that title for many years and has been found useful by many organizations and otherwise by many others. The problem seems to be one of practice and practicality rather than a conceptual one.

In his book *Improving Business Results*, John Humble states the case. "Improving business results [his term for MBO] is a positive approach to improving company profits and growth through the efforts of a competent and purposeful management team." † He states that the method will help a chief executive find practical answers to a number of important questions. It is interesting to see that many of the key questions listed by Humble are similar to the items raised in our chapter on planning, particularly the questions to ask in planning discussed in Chapter 3. These are the types of questions Humble mentions:

- How sound are the objectives and operational plans? Will they enable us to reach long-term goals and improve the profitability of current operations?

*New York: Harper & Row, 1964.
†London: McGraw-Hill, 1967, p. 9.

- Do all parts of the operation understand what they must do?
- Are high-quality resources spending too much time on low opportunity areas?
- Do the managers have the required skills and knowledge, and are they personally motivated and committed?
- What are we planning for the future? What are new sources of income?

These questions are perfectly legitimate and should be part of the activity of any organization, as we showed previously. In practice, most schemes that go under the MBO name have somewhat elaborate plans for obtaining discussion of goals and commitments all along the line. Setting these schemes up takes about two years and works best in more stable industries. Problems may stem from lack of flexibility of many managers and rigid adherence to principles of MBO so that instead of goal-setting being cooperative, it becomes coercive.

Many organizations practice goal-setting and gaining personal commitment without dehumanizing these processes. The problems in some firms may thus reflect inappropriate managerial approaches and not invalidate the concept itself. An organization has to find a human and accountable way to practice managing by setting objectives and keeping tabs on changing objectives. If it looks on an MBO program as a panacea and a mechanical shortcut, it may be making a bad mistake.

COMMUNICATION

We have already discussed aspects of this topic, as it is difficult to avoid doing so when examining the human aspects of management. We now will take a broader look at the subject and then go into specifics in such areas as speaking, holding meetings, and major barriers to proper communication.

Clarity of understanding of the activities of an organization and its overall objectives is essential if there is to be good communication within an organization. If each employee knows the what, why, when, who, and where of his organization, he is better equipped to know what he has to do and to enter into easy and positive communication with others in it. This is a base rock for effective communication.

As we have learned previously, people act on their perceptions, whether these are correct or not. Possibly that is why ideas about communication are most difficult to communicate. Experts on mass communications are the most poorly understood of people. The problem is that the difficulties of achieving good communication are themselves present in every attempt to discuss them. It is something akin to trying to give examples of static noise on a radio broadcast which itself is subject to static noise. Which is the real static and which is the example? Maybe even, which is static static?

A communications setup helps keep the firm with its interdependent parts functioning as a whole. The one-man firm needs to set goals, plan the work, and get it carried out. The communications network in this case is built in. With several managers, a network is not automatically built in; it must be created. It is essential to know what information has to arrive where and when so that the organization functions smoothly. Too much information can be distracting; too little information is like too little oil in machinery.

Information also should not flow like a river through channels. Information has to be digested and interpreted as it moves along the channels. It also must be stored as records to be available when needed. These points are the essence of information distributing.

A proper flow of information is needed to keep the firm on its course. Proper distribution of information acts like feedback in an electrical system. Adjustments are constantly being made to assure a proper following of the direction pointed out by the objectives of the firm.

So far this sounds fairly mechanical. When people are placed in the line of flow of communications—and this is essential at many points—the simple mechanical aspect becomes complex. One has to remember here, too, that there are many other communication setups in any firm aside from the formal ones, and these informal systems can have a vital bearing on the efficiency of a firm.

In communication, the idea is not just to say or write something as we visualize or understand it but to convey a specific meaning to the receiver of that communication. This meaning should tell him what he is expected to do; otherwise, we have not gotten through. The meaning conveyed depends on at least three things: (1) the communication itself, (2) the background and training of the receiver, with all his built-in responses, and (3) the situation in which the transmission takes place.

If we are dealing with direct, face-to-face communication, the situation becomes even more complicated. The words used in the communication are only one part of it. Other factors include the tone of voice, the verbal expression, and the body posture and use of hands. The happy or unhappy frame of mind of the receiver will also have an effect. (This is not as important in written communication, because the reading of a memo could be delayed until the receiver is in a different mood.)

Aristotle had the right idea when he wrote: "It is not enough to know what we are to say; we must say it in the right way." To elaborate on this important point, it is essential, first, that every bit of communication be expressed clearly, even in a totally mechanical setup. The information must be correctly interpreted by the receiver; that is, the receiver must view it as the sender wants it viewed. If an actor works hard at understanding a character in a play, but his projection of this character on a stage is not understood by the audience as he sees it, then that actor has failed to communicate what he had hoped he would. Any message must be considered by the sender in the light of the receiver's possible interpretation of it. One excellent way of achieving a good deal of this in the field of verbal communications is to have the sender carefully listen to what the receiver replies. Listening is not an art for lower echelons; it is essential for all managers. It is almost one of the lost arts.

Other problems of getting information across depend on such matters as the level of sophistication of the receiver. Some specialists can only talk to other specialists. Someone once claimed that they could seat some 30 English professors at a dinner table in such order that nobody would understand what his neighbors were talking about. Maybe you could substitute business school professors here. Certainly you could often substitute a dinner table of managers and those they manage. Specialists are essential; jargons are shortcuts and welcome. But there is a place for them. This, of course, is one major aspect of correctly projecting information.

Trust: An Essential

All this brings in a key point about communication. It works best when there is a feeling of mutual trust and cooperation in an enterprise. When a company is progressing, without people being trampled down in doing so, proper communication is most effective. Here, formal and informal channels reinforce each other. I am not thinking of the happy-family type of company; that may be a sloppy, inefficient firm with a poor profit base. What I mean was probably best expressed long ago in a September 1950 article in *Fortune* magazine entitled "Is Anybody Listening?" The passage is: "Only with trust can there by any real communication, and until trust is achieved, the techniques and gadgetry of communication are so much waste effort." Obviously no great numbers were listening.

In this connection, it is interesting to note the work of TORI Associates in California. The initials stand for trust, openness, realization, and interdependence. Among other things they have developed some methods of measuring the degree of trust (and the other three qualities) in groups. Their groupings include a broader variety than the work organization, and it may not be possible to translate trust as seen in a social or church group to that of a group at paid work. We noted this previously, but some examination of work organizations is part of the practical testing going on.

One of their test instruments, published by University Associates in the 1977 *Annual Handbook for Group Facilitators,** in-

*La Jolla, Calif.: University Associates, Inc., 1977.

cludes a 96-item questionnaire. Organizations are rated with respect to certain statements, using a four-point scale ranging from "strongly disagree" to "strongly agree." The higher the score, the greater the degree of trust in the group. For example, in the following items, an answer of "strongly disagree" rates a score of 3, and down the line to 0 for "strongly agree":

> The members of the group are more interested in getting something done than in caring for each other as individuals.

> People are playing roles in this group and not being themselves.

> Each member of the group seems to play a definite and clear role and is respected on the basis of how well he performs that role.

> It is easy to tell who are the "in" people in this group.

> It is easy to tell who the important members of the group are.

In the next items, the marks go the opposite way; that is, "strongly disagree" now has 0.

> Members of this group trust each other very much.

> People in this group seem to know who they are; they have a real sense of being individuals.

> Members seem to care very much for each other as individuals.

> Group members have a high opinion of my contribution to the group.

> The group treats each person in the group as an important person.*

Language is a strange thing. Perhaps it would be of use to some to recall the words of a great scientist in the field of language, Alfred Korzybski, when he remarked that language is a map of the ideas conceived, not the ideas themselves. When we use a map, we are used to what its purpose is and generally do not get confused. People who rarely use maps can often get well off their desired path

*1977 Annual Handbook for Group Facilitators, pp. 75, 76, and 77.

when they do so. The same thing can happen in the use of language. We do not think of it as a map, but as the thing in itself. It is extremely important to remember this when we are trying to convince an individual of something.

Barriers to Communication

We have seen many barriers to effective communication, and it should prove worthwhile to sum these up or even add a few new ones. Here is a list of the major ones:

- A basic lack of trust between people because of previous experiences.
- Use of jargon that can create confusion. It is either not understood at all or interpreted in a way not meant.
- Too much said about a subject or, for that matter, too little.
- The emotional state of the receiver.
- Poor timing of a message.
- A completely bigoted mind.
- A communicator who doesn't really believe what he is communicating.
- Failure to listen carefully to responses or, in the case of written communications, to monitor them carefully.

Two important items should be added. One, a stereotype approach creates a lack of trust or, sometimes, too much faith. If we think highly of some statesman then we might believe everything he says simply because he says it. Some professions such as professors or doctors, have—or used to have—an aura of intelligence; thus, when they speak, we tend to believe them. On the other hand, if we are politically conservative, we might not believe anything some radical tells us, even though he might be saying something very significant and useful. The same thing of course holds the other way around. Two, an arrogant approach—invariably assuming the other person must be mistaken, since we know better— will generally forestall communication. A smaller version of this is our tendency to forget what we don't agree with and recall that which we do agree with. This fortifies a personal feeling of being right but can sometimes be disastrous.

Overcoming the Barriers

Each item in this list of communication barriers gives clues to how to overcome them. And the greatest way to do so is to get feedback. This requires listening skills—the ability to say nothing but carefully listen to what someone else is saying (or writing) or even conveying in the tone of voice or the posture of the body. Feedback is vital if communication is to be effective. It might call for people to repeat information which they have just heard to see if sender and receiver are agreeing. Often it is useful for a receiver of information to say: "What you are telling me is . . ." or "What you wish me to do is. . . ."

An interesting exercise for a group of people would be to select a few current topics on, say, politics or social affairs and to have each person select a topic and jot down a few notes on this subject. The group can then divide into pairs. One person will talk on his subject for some three to five minutes using his notes. The other person will listen but make no notes. New pairs will then be formed until each individual has heard some three talks by other members as well as given his own talk a few times. A listener will then repeat the contents of the first talk he hears as he recalls it. This can be done to the group, some of whom have heard the same talk. There is no interruption when a listener is reporting. Afterward, others can say what they believe was missed or reported incorrectly. It is amazing to find that there are so many poor listeners among our friends or associates—including ourselves.

Listening becomes critical when we are in a discussion on a subject. We are often so anxious to express our own point of view that we hardly listen to what anyone else is saying. We only wait for an opportunity to jump in and say what is on our minds. If this happens, as it often does, when a manager is talking to a subordinate (and vice versa), no wonder something goes wrong afterward.

Speaking

One of the most useful things for a person to learn is the ability to speak to a group. It is extremely useful if a manager—and not only a sales manager—can make a proper presentation. We may never become great after-dinner speakers or be able to address large crowds in many places for an hour or more at a time. But all people in organizations have to talk to members of their group or to several groups from time to time. Some of these talks should be prepared and well presented. Doing this will even rub off on the countless informal sessions in which people in many organizations participate from time to time.

It is easy to think of some people as born speakers. Hearing them at meetings or over TV, it appears to be a natural gift. And if we haven't got it, then too bad. However, most can acquire some real ability in this field. Like most things it requires preparation and work. When the great sculptor and painter Michelangelo was congratulated on his mastery of his art and his magnificent ability, he replied: "If people knew how hard I have to work to gain my mastery, it would not seem wonderful at all."

The problem with many managers is that they will not work at being managers, and so they rarely become good ones. This problem is not restricted to managers; it is true of others. Many artists will not work at their craft, nor will many lawyers, accountants, teachers, and professors. The result is that, although many are inherently capable of becoming great in their fields, few do. Most of those who do, work at it; the odd one sneaks through by some chance.

The intention here is not to provide a step-by-step guide on how to become a capable speaker. We will focus instead on the main aspects to be considered in making a presentation—or even a long speech—and those who wish can study and work at it.

Making a good presentation has six major aspects, with some overlapping between them. Here they are, with some ideas on how to analyze each.

Material—has the material proper objective, organization, use of research, illustrations, etc? Does it have proper body, with start, middle and end, or is it just a collection of items? Sentence structure generally good, use of words intelligent?

Projection of ideas—does the basic idea come through easily; are the facts assembled logically to make them easily understood? Does the audience feel involvement and satisfaction?

Speaking personality—does the speaker appear at ease and friendly and really interested in what he has to say and in his audience? Do his voice and body activities underscore his meaning or distract from it?

Body movements—are movements jerky, indecisive, useless, distracting? Do they help ideas or hinder understanding of them?

Voice—is it too high, too low, monotonous, or harsh, or is it pleasant and pitched correctly? Do sentences drop away or finish cleanly? Are there "ahs" and "hmmns"?

Clarity of speaking—are words clearly understandable? Are sentences distinct, or do they blur into each other? In short, can you clearly understand each word?

These areas are not of equal importance. If *material* is scored on a basis of 25 points being excellent and 0 points being poor, then *projection of ideas* could also have a 0 to 25 scale, *speaking personality* a 0 to 20 scale, and the final three a 0 to 10 scale.

A person very poor in *voice* or *clarity of speaking* would be difficult to listen to, but if all the other scores were high, then listeners would discount some of these superficial problems with diction. They can be worked on like all the others. Body movements would also depend on the size of an audience. In a large crowd, forceful body movements would be called for and accepted, but they might look somewhat exaggerated in a small group. Each of the items calls for preparation and practice.

Meetings

Edward de Bono, the witty writer and lecturer on creative thinking, wrote in one of his early books, *Practical Thinking,* * "Thinking is that waste of time between seeing something and knowing what to do about it." It is a witty, tongue-in-cheek observation.

*London: Jonathan Cape, 1971, p. 13.

Unfortunately, what happens between seeing something and knowing what to do about it is that people hold many meetings. And many of these are really a waste of time. It is one of the most common areas for complaints in all organizations. Meetings are obviously essential for the proper functioning of an organization. The trouble arises because so few people appear to know how to arrange and conduct a good meeting.

One poor meeting begets another, for if it is poorly arranged in the first place, there frequently needs to be another meeting scheduled to pick up some of the pieces, and then another one, and so on. If half the meetings held in work organizations were properly prepared for and properly conducted, there is little doubt that management productivity would go up a good 10 percent or more. (That figure is a guess. Maybe I should call a meeting to discuss the topic and try to obtain a better figure.)

Arranging for and conducting a meeting is an important management skill, yet in training for management it is generally overlooked or looked down upon as a minor skill. Any skill which can save an organization a good slice of money over a month or a year is hardly a minor skill. If any large organization did an accounting of the number of hours each manager spent at meetings and considered the extra hours of work before and after a meeting, then multiplied the hours by the hourly pay rate of the people present, the sum would be shocking. Even a 10 percent saving would be welcome.

Interestingly enough, the method of preparing for and conducting a good meeting is exactly the same as preparing for and conducting good management in an organization. It requires planning, organizing, staffing, directing, and controlling—the very same activities we are considering in this text as the basic management functions. This holds even if the meeting is a simple, fast get-together to consider some immediate problem that has developed, such as a loss of power in a production unit of a manufacturing concern or an immediate request for some type of action by a senior department or outside organization. Unfortunately, many meetings are held where the purpose and other aspects of the meetings are not nearly as clear.

Under planning, we are concerned with the objective of the meeting. Is there a problem to discuss, a situation of concern to the organization? An equally valid objective could be to address a morale problem, where a meeting is held to state the facts of a situation about which there is or could be all sorts of rumors.

Know what the objective is—and there can be several—and then determine what background information is required. What work has to be done to assemble this information? Are specialists required for consultation? How long will it take to get the information together? How much time is there to do it? Already the meeting is beginning to look like a practical and useful working operation and not a pooling of ignorance, as is so often the case.

Knowing all this also helps us plan for the type of space we require and the equipment we might need, and it alerts people to do some homework of their own. We also obtain an idea of what will be the structure of the meeting. How much time do we need for presentation? Should material be sent out to attendants in advance for study? How much time do we have for discussion? Knowing the objective(s) and that we are trying to reach some conclusion(s) or come to some understanding or make some first approximation about a major problem, we are planning the utilization of the results of the meeting.

In a sense we have already impinged on organizing, but that is the problem in management in general—the functions bump into each other frequently, because they are so interrelated.

In staffing, we need to see which people must be present and what others should be present. Should a chairperson be appointed right from the start or should one be selected at the meeting? If so, how will this be done? We must also see to it that all the staff people or others whose opinions are required do their work for the meeting.

Under directing, we are concerned with creating an interest in discussion, and we can create an interest before, during, and after the meeting. We consider ways to motivate various people to contribute and how to deal with them when they do. Under controlling, we follow the plan. This tells what constraints are on the group. Does it make any decision it feels it should? Who else then has a say in what happens? Are there financial constraints? Legal constraints that some might not be aware of?

And the final and eternal question: what do we do to follow up on things and on people? If we notice reactions and attitudes of some attendees, should we follow this up or move the decisions on to the next stage? If we are concerned with people, then we would certainly follow up with discussions with some individuals, depending on what transpired at the meeting.

All this sounds like an elaborate preparation for a minor affair. In practice, if we use the pattern of the management functions, much can fall in place fairly easily. For important meetings, preparation time is vital if the meeting is not to flounder and then lead to other meetings because someone forgot to prepare some important material or to speak to some individual who has an interesting, perhaps vital, contribution to make.

The actual conducting of the meeting is difficult to cover in short order. Going through the process as spelled out here and keeping in mind what type of people will be present will give clues to this. If the major points covered in Chapter 2, which dealt with the human aspects of management, are taken into consideration, we should have some strong feeling for how this is to be done. To follow elaborate parliamentary procedures or the details of some book of rules would be fine for a major and large meeting, but will probably bog down most smaller meetings. Discussion in general should be free-flowing, democratic, and to the point, whether it is exactly according to Hoyle or not.

The basic approach to conducting a meeting involves the two areas of critical concern discussed under leadership in Chapter 2. The person chairing a meeting must have a real concern for the tasks involved in the meeting. What are the objectives? But he has to be equally concerned with people. One might ram home decisions at meetings in order to obtain a feeling of accomplishment, but this feeling will be short-lived if few understand and really agree with the decisions. People at meetings should not be asked to discuss items on which their decisions will have no impact. The group either has no authority in the area of the subject, or somebody upstairs doesn't really give a damn about what others say on a topic and is going to do what he thinks he should regardless. Statements that this is not the case will fall flat after a time if the reality is otherwise.

The chairperson or leader of the meeting has to act as a good manager and listen to what is going on and determine, among other things:

- When there is a need to clarify a point.
- When certain items should be focused on.
- When he or someone else should be requested to summarize a discussion.
- When he should try to get a decision made and also when he should not try to force a decision.
- When people are bringing special biases and have their own private hidden agendas for a meeting—and how best to bring this fact out into the open without necessarily naming people.
- When real issues must be faced, even if they lead to heat and controversy.
- When feelings should be allowed open expression because they are facts that will influence the implementation of the decisions to be made.
- When to bring silent members into the act without placing them on the spot. This may require a good understanding of body language as well as knowledge of the person.
- When and how to silence individuals who like to dominate a meeting either out of a need for power and recognition or because of strong personal biases.
- How to deal with clowning if it becomes too pronounced.

Aside from being concerned with the tasks set for the meeting, the chairperson is also concerned with maintaining good working order in the group and paying careful attention to people's needs. This leads to building a good organizational climate where team work is considered interesting and useful to all.

Written communications follow the same general guidelines discussed for meetings. A major point to remember is that written communications do not have the very useful accompaniment of nonverbal aspects, which are extremely important. Thus more emphasis is placed on the actual words used. Feedback is also slowed down, for one cannot simply say: "What you are saying is . . ." or something similar. Written communications can, of course, be checked and changed, if necessary. They have special value in that they remain as a document to refer back to and, of course, as a guide when they give instructions or outline a plan. Taped conversations, although useful, would not be as effective.

A key point, then, in using written communications is to pay attention to words and sentences. They should be basically simple and short. Some amount of redundancy should also be built in, such as happens normally in speech. Redundancy assures a better understanding of the message, because it can correct a first false interpretation.

Questions for Review

1. Give some examples of communications, both written and oral, that have gone astray, and give your reasons why this has happened.

_____

_____

_____

_____

2. Score yourself on the group trust items, using the group in which you work as the basis for the marks.

On the first five items, scoring is:	Strongly Disagree 3	Disagree 2	Agree 1	Strongly Agree 0
1.				
2.				
3.				
4.				
5.				
Subtotal _____				

On the second five items scoring is:	Strongly Disagree 0	Disagree 1	Agree 2	Strongly Agree 3
1.				
2.				
3.				
4.				
5.				
Subtotal ____				
Total ____				

The highest possible score on these questions is 30.

3. What do you find are the basic barriers to communications?

_____

_____

4. Has your listening ability improved over the past year?
Yes_____ No_____
If yes, explain why you think so, including any efforts you made to improve it. If no, what do you think of yourself as a listener?
Very good_____ good_____ fair_____poor_____ very poor_____
5. What are the main items a person should consider when giving a talk?

_____

_____

_____

6. Recall some talks that you have heard recently (not on radio or TV) and evaluate them on the preceding criteria.

_____

_____

_____

_____

7. Reread the Zedline Company case and your comments on it and explain how you would prepare for a meeting after the investigating committee had made major progress. Draw up the agenda.

COUNSELING

Counseling is important work for managers. They should be able to deal positively and effectively with the problems faced by people working for them. These problems should be work-related. Some managers feel the need to listen to and advise people on their personal problems. In many cases personal problems do affect work on the job itself, but unless a manager is fully trained to counsel people on their personal problems, he would be well advised not to do so. Most managers do not have the competencies required for giving personal advice.

It is hard—and probably wrong—to shut a worker off when he brings up a personal problem. Managers probably have to be good listeners at this point. However, they should steer people to the proper community services rather than try to give too much non-work-related advice.

Although a manager should have some sympathy for the problems faced by those he deals with as a manager, including personal problems, his basic role is to have empathy. He should understand the individual, be able to put himself in the other person's shoes. If he goes beyond that, then he changes the relationship between himself and those who work with him. He may start making and accepting excuses for poor performance rather than try to make the changes necessary to improve performance.

There are two major counseling methods and an intermediate stage. They are:

Directive counseling—the boss controls the situation, asks questions, often provides possible excuses. This does not often lead to the real sources of problems.

Nondirective counseling—there is no attempt here to create a boss-subordinate type of relationship but an attempt to stimulate insight. It starts with tension release and leads to development of insights and formation of new plans. Listening is a key ingredient here. Negative feelings are drawn out without forcing an agreement, and then real problems are discussed. This method generally leads to results.

However, there may be a time and a place for each method, depending on the situation. Generally a mixture of two is used.

Cooperative counseling—a mixture of directive and nondirective methods.

There are several other items to observe when carrying on counseling:

Do it in a quiet place where there will be no interruptions.
Prepare for the session with necessary facts.
Have empathy, realize differences in the way the two of you
    may look at things.
Focus as much as possible on things done correctly.
Remember to listen.
Remember what nonverbal signals might show.
Try to figure out if Parent, Adult, or Child is speaking.

Reviewing Counseling Sessions

After a counseling session it is a wise idea to review the notes on it by asking questions such as:

Did the person with the problem do most of the talking during the session, or did he or she mainly listen? If the latter is the case, then there is something wrong with the way the manager handles counseling.

What did the manager do to help the subordinate explain what the problem was, including his feelings about it? If the manager did help, then the manager should have obtained a look at the problem as the other person perceived it. This is essential. It is very difficult to conduct a session successfully unless the perceptions are understood.

Did the employee give any real evidence that his problem was correctly understood by the manager? This may not be an easy question to answer, for an employee may be intimidated even if that is not the intention of the manager. The employee may also feel that his problem is understood simply because he has a sympathetic manager to talk to. In this latter case, the battle may be half won, which is probably an accomplishment of some worth.

In dealing with the employee, did the manager use direct questions? Did he probe into the situation in order to gather more information to make sure he was getting at the kernel of the situation? Did the manager offer some reflections on the situation which could lead to new insights and further statements by the employee?

Looking at some negative possibilities, one could ask if the manager tried to argue and interrupt the employee as he was explaining his views. Some managers feel that to control a counseling session (which they should), they must mastermind the situation and come to a solution or answer which is verbally accepted—but not really accepted inside. To control the interview is to probe and sympathize in order to obtain all the facts and feelings essential in the situation. It does not mean to browbeat an employee, whether the manager sees himself as a prosecuting attorney or not.

A final question to ask is, who came up with a positive solution, if one was reached at the session? If it emerged from the employee as he began to see the problem more clearly and recognized that he was not being purposely discriminated against, the solution is much more likely to be effective.

APPRAISAL AND EVALUATION

One of the most important sessions between a manager and those who work for him takes place when a subordinate is being appraised and his performance on the job evaluated. Such interviews should take place separately from those concerning salaries. When a union is involved, this probably happens anyway. The discussion should be open and frank, and opinions recorded and witnessed. Evaluations should not be secretive, with the employee learning only half truths about his performance on the job.

However, the regular appraisal and evaluation interview is only one part of the process. We must first make sure we know:

• What skills and knowledge are being evaluated?
• What standards are there in the required skills and knowledge?
• What followup takes place in order to obtain improvement?

A simple approach might be based on the following form:

Name_____ Dept._____

Evaluation_____

Item Being Evaluated	Poor	Adequate	Good
1. _____	_____	_____	_____
2. _____	_____	_____	_____
3. _____	_____	_____	_____

This could easily be made more sophisticated. A highly useful way to look at this subject stems from the DACUM approach. The word stands for *Developing a Curriculum*. We used some of these basic ideas in the recruiting section where we talked about the competencies required in a job and the knowledge and skills minimally required to do the work plus the levels needed to do the job adequately or extremely well.

It is useful to illustrate this approach with an example. The one we'll use concerns the position of professional counselor in a school system and is taken from a book* prepared by R. E. Adams.

The competencies required for the professional school counselor were figured out to be:

Communicate.
Identify and specify problems and student needs.
Apply counseling methods.
Apply special group counseling methods.
Measure and evaluate.
Serve as consultant.
Apply behavior change techniques.
Administer program of services.
Organize and conduct vocational and educational information programs.
Enlist and utilize community referral resources.
Employ effective instruction techniques.
Develop and implement programs in psychological education.
Continue to acquire professional competence.

*DACUM Approach to Curriculum, Learning and Evaluation in Occupational Training, 2nd ed. A Nova Scotia Newsstand Report. Ottawa: Department of Regional Economic Expansion of Canada, 1975.

Each of these 13 items was then broken down into more specific pieces of information. This produced several dozen items. Under "apply counseling methods," for example, are such items as "conduct role playing sessions," "advise, persuade, and influence," "terminate counseling process or treatment," "share feeling and experience with client," "encourage and direct expressions of feelings," "interpret client's behavior to client," and "develop sense of responsibility in client." Each one of these detailed items was evaluated on a seven-point scale. This scale is most useful and instructive. Here it is, with some omissions:

> *0* shows that the individual cannot perform the specific task satisfactorily for participation in a work environment.

> *1* indicates the person can perform the task but requires constant supervision and occasional assistance.

> *2* indicates that performance is satisfactory but the individual requires regular supervision and help.

> *3* shows that the task can now be carried out without assistance and supervision.

> . . .

> *6* shows that not only is level *5* achieved but the person can lead others in the performance of the task.

By breaking the job into this multitude of tasks, one can judge the skill level of an individual from period to period. This permits a manager to show individuals where they stand in their work and where they still have to go. The DACUM approach does not eliminate the need to evaluate the performance of any individual, but it provides a more rational approach to the process of evaluation and makes much more specific in what respects the individual has to improve if he wishes to go up.

Appraisal Interviews

The approach just discussed simplifies the appraisal interview if such information is kept in some form of chart, with skill levels added in at the dates on which they are accomplished. However, it does not eliminate the interview or the need for personal assessment.

The appraisal interview may be of the kind: "This is where I think you stand now on your job. You got the ability to move up, so go in there and fight to raise your ratings." This is the tell-and-sell interview. Or it may go something like: "This is where I think you stand now on your job. You've done quite well. Now what are you going to do?" Here we have the tell-and-listen interview. Or it can be: "This is where I judge you to stand now on your job. You are doing well, but there is still room to grow in many areas. What are some of the problems you are experiencing in moving up? Let's examine the specific areas." This is the problem-solving interview.

As should be clear from the material developed in Chapter 2, the third type of interview is the preferred one. It is also best used in conjunction with the evaluation method we have discussed. Unfortunately, this is not often the case. Many evaluation methods grade an individual on several broad items such as quantity of work, quality of work, ability to get along, and ability to help others, and, furthermore, use an inadequate rating scale. The first two items—quantity and quality of work—can be vague unless buttressed by such information as provided by the DACUM approach, which focuses on relevant specifics. In dealing with an employee, it is necessary to discuss specifics rather than generalities. While there must also be some information on ability to work with people built into an evaluation—if this ability is required— using only general information places an evaluation on the wrong foot at the start.

The basic idea of the interview is to improve performance. (We mentioned keeping the salary aspect to a separate time, but obviously salary is related to performance.) Therefore, we approach the interview as one designated to help the individual being appraised. The manager is not sitting in judgment and pointing out how a worker can improve. If he does so, he builds up defenses, worsens motivation, and generally ends with a less committed and rarely an improved worker. If the manager expects the subordinate to take charge of the interview at once—that is, if he takes the tell-and-listen approach—he is not performing his job as a manager.

He may help improve performance somewhat by adopting a relatively free and easy style, but he is not giving his evaluation and pointing up possible changes and getting them accepted by the employee. This can be particularly true when he does not have specifics on which to base his interview and evaluation. When he approaches the interview as a problem-solving situation and uses the evaluation method we have discussed, he not only starts off on the right foot with specifics but continues on that way by working with the individual to improve performance. This vastly increases the chance of developing more motivation, more commitment, and a better performance in the future.

A manager's human judgment has not been bypassed in the evaluation procedures. His judgment is extremely important even when he uses the DACUM levels of proficiency. What these do is give him the rational information required to make a decision; this must be supplemented by the manager's gut feelings about the ability of the performer.

Without this type of classification scheme, a manager is thrown back on memory of major incidents and use of his intuitive feelings. We do not wish to eliminate human intuition, as it is most important. However, we have pointed out a number of times that intuition backed by conscious evaluation of a worker using useful techniques is the best approach. Gut feelings, without examining a situation as analytically as possible first, can be just an excuse for laziness. A DACUM evaluation approach, or any other conceptually similar systematic method, provides an analytic and conscious method of approaching an appraisal, at the same time stimulating the intuitive capacities to their highest state.

In brief, human judgment is still the important fact in appraisal, as it is in all decision making by managers. But it should best come not just out of the blue, but backed by some intelligent scheme.

TRAINING AND DEVELOPMENT

An organization should make use of education in recruiting people required to serve its needs. Internal training and development activities should enable employees to do their jobs more effectively and to acquire and develop abilities and skills necessary to carry out activities at a higher level in the organization, or to adapt to new skills and abilities needed to meet the changing requirements of the organization itself. Often organizations do not know enough about what skills and abilities are required of them today and tomorrow or about the skills, abilities, and potential of the people already working for them.

Training and development should be thought of as management tools essential for the improvement of the operations of the organization. Managers, unfortunately, in many cases think of education as something removed from the organization—something that might at best help people to help the organization. Thus training and development are often left to specialists or to outside organizations, whether educational institutions or private firms, while managers pray for changes.

The responsibility for training and development belongs to the line manager; it is part of his activities in being a manager. He brings in the specialists—educational institution or otherwise—to help him do the work, just as he might bring in mechanical specialists to improve some equipment in a plant operation. The manager uses education to get better performance out of an organization.

One of the problems might be the word education itself, which conjures up visions of sitting in classrooms, listening to lectures, and waiting for the session to end. Education is beyond that, in reality. A manager helping his staff understand a problem or a situation that has arisen is acting as an educator in the best sense of the word. He is helping people *to use knowledge,* not just to acquire it. His own personal development should provide him with some information on what learning is all about and how to make use of the most effective means for his training and development purposes.

By now we can see a strong link between knowing what constitutes a job, how to appraise a person working at a job, and making use of the best training activities to improve the individual skills, whether this takes place on the job itself or in something resembling a classroom. There are three basic parts to this activity: preparation, training sessions, and followup.

Under preparation, we are concerned with determining the what and why of the knowledge or the skills to be acquired or honed, and the current level of these in the workforce designated to undertake the training. We are also concerned with individual fears about undergoing training, particularly if it is to consist of some classroom sessions. The preparation is basically the same whether a manager is seeking to help one individual with some aspect of his work or picking out a group of people who need improvement in their performances or are being given new knowledge and skills because of changes in their position or changes taking place in the organization itself.

On the basis of this information, or needs analysis, which is concerned not only with the specifics of what is to be taught but also with the level of skills of the trainees and their perceptions and feeling about training, a program is developed to suit the needs. The word program may be too big for a manager spending a short time with one individual, but the idea is the same. When a program is developed or used for a group of people and takes place over some time, and outsiders—either from other parts of the organization or outside it—are brought in to conduct sessions, the manager is still responsible for the results. Therefore, he has to be directly concerned with what is going on in training.

Followup is essential if we are going to effect the desired changes in people and their performance. We either succeed, wholly or in part, or we don't succeed at all. In the first case, we can feel happy for the moment. The managers check to see that what was supposedly learned is being applied correctly. They reinforce this by approval and help on the job to see that what has been learned becomes an integral part of the individual's practice at work. If we omit this last part, we forget a major activity in training and development.

In practice, many people are exposed to training programs without any preparation except a general understanding that it could be good and helpful to the individual. When that individual finishes some of the training and gets back on the job, often little use or demand is made for the skills or knowledge supposedly acquired. This is true in management much more often than in training involving lower-level skills. Training and development is a continuous thing in any manager's life. He is carrying on with it on the job, arranging special sessions when these are required, and he follows up because the name of the game is improving on-the-job performance. The whole process is repeated in small or large form over time. Like breathing, there is no end to it.

Training Can Create Problems, Too

Training that has been undertaken for its own sake can lead to problems. This is well illustrated in the following situation. The personnel manager of an organization of several hundred workers was an older man near retirement who paid little attention to new thinking about organization and carried on a "hiring shop," with other clerical aspects of personnel work thrown in. A younger man was hired as a personnel assistant, though it was expected that he would do the actual job. Lack of knowledge about modern personnel practices by senior managers led to the hiring of an individual who was anxious to have the job but who, upon later examination, proved to have no real background in the field and no knowledge of what to do about salary administration and other personnel matters.

The personnel assistant decided to ask a university to conduct a management course for supervisors in the organization. This, the personnel assistant felt, would lead to discussions about other aspects of his job with supposedly knowledgeable university people and allow him to obtain some of the information he desired.

The university approached said yes, it could put on a supervisory management program for supervisors and would be able to send instructors into the organization's own offices. An effort was made by the university to fit a general supervisory training program to the organization's needs. The usual meetings were held with instructors to discuss content and approach, and finally a 16-

week course, with meetings once a week, was carried on, involving about 80 first-line supervisors.

When the university analyzed the effectiveness of the program in this organization and held subsequent talks with the assistant director of personnel, the full story came out. Briefly, this man showed his inabilities to his supervisors very quickly and was fired even before the course was over.

The course went on its way and revealed a number of problems in this organization. Much of the new thinking of the personnel involved in the course was brought about by the understanding of management which they obtained from the course. The students began to think of their own organization in the light of their learning and soon perceived a great many inadequacies in their own organization. Questioning of these students at the end revealed some very interesting information.

This firm obviously needed a good training and development program, but a hard look at the organization should have come first. Training is an integral part of the activities of any company. Yet the senior executives who approved the program, the assistant personnel director who pushed for it to be given, and the university which had developed and given it never saw the full meaning of education in an organization. The elephant had various meanings for each. The internal strife and dissatisfaction which brewed in the company made many unhappy until a more sensible approach was finally undertaken.

The last paragraph brings out a point which has been mentioned in other chapters: that we should first think of how an organization can be changed to suit its employees, and second, how the latter may be made to fit an organization. There is little need to train people for certain changes if these changes can be accomplished better by changing the organization itself. This will not do away with much training and development activity in any organization, but it is a point to be considered.

Finally, a good question to ask is, is this training necessary? Or can the organization's objectives be accomplished without it? Cost could also be a factor in the situation.

Learning

Since a great deal of a manager's work is involved with training, either individually or in small groups, he should have some knowledge and feeling for the learning process. He should realize that it does not take place continuously but more often in spurts, and periods where no learning appears to be taking place occur in between. The goal of training and development is change by providing additional information, correcting incorrect information, and adding or improving skills. The process is carried on when required in the organization so that the information or skill can be utilized right after it is acquired.

Real learning requires *involvement*. This is why many "resisting" adults prefer lectures and handouts and a back seat in a classroom. Even if their fears are only imaginary, they do not want their self-image threatened. To obtain a person's involvement, a manager needs to have some good idea of the individual's perceptions of the need for learning and change. He should also start with what the individual knows and build on that information. Learning is thus a two-way street, not something handed down from instructor to pupil. Unless there is real involvement, the chances that the learning will be internalized are limited.

A very major reason why the training role of managers is important is because most adults really prefer to learn on their own. They acquire ideas from books they read, from friends and from colleagues. It is a much slower process than organized learning, but since many people are more comfortable with it, it cannot be neglected. One way to do so is to try to convert this self-learning into what educator Malcolm S. Knowles terms "self-directed" learning. In essence the process is like helping a person set goals for himself in an organization. Here, with the help of a manager or someone designated for this purpose by a manager, a person sets training and development goals for himself. He is aided to discover all possible sources of help, including books, articles, seminars of all types, people in the organization, and people in associations. He then proceeds on his own after a careful discussion of what he is attempting to accomplish. He may and should check back with his "facilitator" to discuss items and other sources of help, as well as to see how he is progressing. This approach permits a person to function on his own so that he may feel more comfortable and accomplish his learning needs by his own life style rather than in an organized classroom—at least not all the time.

Instructor Problems

In formal or even informal sessions, whether a manager acts as a teacher himself or utilizes others for this purpose, he should be aware of and guard against problems of teachers, such as:

- A tendency to act as a controller of people and make them dependent on the teacher.
- A need for affection that may distort the learning process. (This should not rule out a little ham in an instructor, but not if it becomes a show.)
- A lack of arm's length approach. People should not be repressed in order to avoid a hot discussion, nor should there be favorites because of personal likes or dislikes. The instructor's job is to facilitate the learning process, not to love everybody in the class.

While it is relatively simple to note these problems, there is also the fact that some instructors do not see themselves as others see them in class. Like all of us, they act by their own perceptions of themselves. If some of the above-mentioned problems occur, they may not be understood by the instructor, and he may have to be helped to perceive them or be replaced as an instructor.

Learning Aids for Instructor–Managers

Here are some techniques and ideas that are useful to remember for a teaching situation:

Tell them the subject matter first, then summarize at the end.

Associate one idea with one other known one.

Discuss ideas in small packages.

Vivid learning experiences are better remembered.

Correct practice makes perfect.

Repeat material.

Let people work through problems by themselves; don't always worry about temporary confusion.

Praise wherever possible.

Have people aware of how they are doing, as much as possible. Feedback is essential for change.

Learning a skill, or knowledge only, is well retained if used and practiced.

Questions for Review

1. Name and describe the various main methods of counseling and briefly comment on their value.

_____

_____

_____

_____

2. If you were silently observing a counseling session, how would you go about estimating its success?

_____

_____

_____

3. Describe a counseling session that you have experienced or know about and comment on how it was handled and whether or not it lead to some measure of success.

_____

_____

_____

4. What are the main steps in carrying out appraisals of performance, and why are they carried out?

_____

_____

_____

_____

5. What knowledge and skills are required by a person in a position similar to yours? (First name the position.)

_____

_____

_____

_____

6. Name the main kinds of appraisal interviews and comment on each.

_____

_____

_____

_____

7. What is the purpose of and basic approach to carrying out training and development activities?

_____

_____

_____

8. Select a manager who in your opinion demonstrates some deficiencies on his job and develop what you think would be a good educational program, including on-the-job training, coaching (a form of counseling), and seminars. Allow a year's time for the activities.

_____

_____

_____

9. What training have you taken under the auspices of your organization which have given you knowledge and skills not used afterward? (If not yourself, use the experiences of someone you know.) How did this happen?

_____

_____

_____

_____

10. What basic ideas about learning should a manager know before conducting a training program (whether or not he gives all the sessions)?

_____

_____

_____

_____

_____

CONTROLLING

Having gone through the gamut of planning, organizing, staffing, and directing an organization, there is one more obvious essential, and that is making sure that the system works. In other words, we have to control the setup we have created.

In discussing organization in Chapter 4, we noted that setting up an organization involves obtaining the necessary resources, human and material, and so ordering and integrating them that people in the organization can carry out their assigned tasks and achieve the desired results. This must be accomplished within deadlines set for the work, within financial budgets, within the quality desired in the outputs, and following the methods and procedures set out by the policies of the organization.

The job of doing these things comes under controlling. It wraps up the package of management functions, making sure that plans and objectives which are carried out over time keep on course, or, at worst, we know when they go off course and corrective actions might be undertaken as well as adjustments made to meet new deadlines. Without careful planning we cannot have proper controls.

Given planning with goals, the first point to be decided in controlling activities is at what main points controls should be set up. There is little point in controlling all activities, since much of the information obtained would overlap. Only strategic points should be checked. Instituting too many controls would be costly, and there is no advantage if more money is spent on a controlling system than is gained by having it. The key control points will vary from organization to organization and may include checking profits, inventory levels, availability of cash, numbers and types of people employed, growth of managers, and turnover, among others.

With the vital areas determined by the manager or managers of an operation, the next thing is to set up ways of knowing whether the operation is on course or not. This requires the development of standards and tolerances in the selected control points. This operation is similar in idea to checking standards and tolerances in a manufacturing operation. A manufacturer of cheap radios may use a simple ''it works or it doesn't work'' idea after the set is put together. In the making of big ticket items, many of the component parts will be checked before the final product is itself checked. Otherwise, there would be costly wastage in the production of these items.

Many of the standards are, or depend on, the objectives set for the organization. If percentages of growth are set, then controls must be instituted to see if these percentages are achieved. Thus, as we have stated before, planning and controlling are intimately connected. When deviations from the standard are noted, then corrections have to be made. Sometimes corrections are automatically made, as deviations become known as regular ones; other times senior management is consulted to determine the course of action. The course of action may require correction of activities so as to achieve the standard, or it may require changing the standard. This is part of management by exception.

In the process of checking standards and effecting corrections, time is involved. We have not stated it explicitly so far, but it should be obvious that corrections should be made as soon as possible. Having information about a deviation long after the deviation has started is of little use. Any control system has to take into account the time between finding out what is happening and making the correction. Also implicit is that idea that control information should point up the area where there is trouble. It should indicate at what point or points there are weaknesses developing and what person or persons are responsible.

The operation of controls must frequently be concerned with human relations. A system of control which some managers use is to sample incoming mail on a regular basis. If the mail is small, the whole of it might be read by a senior manager. This helps keep the manager on top of what is happening in the firm. However, it might also destroy personnel relations in the firm. Though a manager is responsible for what his juniors do and say in the name of the firm, continual over-the-shoulder peeking could limit creativity in some areas, making conformists out of some people who could contribute better to the firm.

Considering the enterprise as a system, attention should be paid to feedback. A proper flow of information is needed to keep the firm on its course. Proper distribution of information acts like feedback in an electrical system. Adjustments must constantly be made to assure proper following of the direction pointed out by the objectives of the firm.

Budgeting

From the preceding discussion it should be obvious that proper budgeting is an important aspect of the control function. It is not the intention here to go into any detail of the budgeting process, since that is an exhaustive subject on its own. Budgets give control because, if accounting is adequate, we can quickly realize that things are going out of line, pinpoint the departure areas in many cases, and decide what action to take on the situation. Cost budgets will also reflect people problems. Some of them may be simple—say, too much hiring was done on a certain job, or too many skilled and more highly paid workers were used than was necessary.

Budgets are automatic if properly kept up and in many cases can be computerized. Inventory control on a computer can even cut costs itself. As items move out of stock, this information is passed on to the computer, which subtracts it from the amount previously noted. The computer is coded for reorder levels as well as for danger points should one big deletion take it well below a safe, normal reorder level. By quick controls of this sort, total stock can be kept below what is usually the practice in handling inventories, and this means more money saved in itself. For smaller operations a computerized control system is not necessary, but the thinking going into the control system is the same.

The new use of zero-base budgeting is in itself a control system. It forces rethinking of what is being done to see what is essential and what is not so essential. It can be used in businesses as well as government organizations. It does require a lot of paper work to start with and thus a lot of time at the beginning. The basic idea is to determine the lowest acceptable level for a department or organization in total. What is the smallest budget required to keep the outfit alive and functioning? To this are added all new costs, but these must be justified as fulfilling certain of the objectives and being the best way to fulfill them.

This sharp rethinking is particularly useful when a branch or group has been functioning for some time and budgeting proceeds mainly as an add-on feature (What growth do you expect this year? Ten percent? Then add on 10 percent plus whatever to allow for inflation.) It can function as an overall control method for any organization that has started to operate with too much fat on its objectives and has reached a state of comfortable flabbiness.

Feedback

It is obvious that in all control systems, quick feedback is essential. Without this any control system soon breaks down. Most computerized control systems have built-in immediate feedback—

though it doesn't always work. Other systems use feedback methods dependent on people supplying information along proper channels as soon as it is required.

One of the basic reasons feedback is often not as good as it should be is that the control systems are generally based on jargon developed by those who build the system, whether they are accountants or systems specialists. Fortunately a new order of individual is arising who focuses on how the user of the system perceives what he is doing and why he is doing it, rather than on the gobbledygook which appears to brainbrand so many specialists.

Salesmen are traditionally antagonistic to reporting-back methods. Often this is because the accountant or marketing manager behind them thinks in terms of specialist jargon and what he and/or the head office requires from the information rather than how to get the supplier of the information to give it more easily.

This point brings us around to a most important aspect of any control system in any organization. This is an understanding of what's going on and a feeling of importance in helping supply information by those who work in the system. An understanding, cooperative group of people, whether workers on the line or people at management levels, with trust in the operation and some sense of commitment to it, is the best control system of all. It will reduce costs more than any fancy, sophisticated techniques. With it the techniques—which are in themselves worthwhile—will function well; without it, the fancy systems will not function nearly as well and can often be as lacking in real use as are many reports hastily filled in by salespeople under compulsion to ship figures up the management line.

THE GENERAL SYSTEMS APPROACH

The systems approach to management simply means applying a scientific approach to the study of an organization to see how its parts work together to produce results and how the organization is related to its environment. The aim is to provide an understandable account of how an organization functions so that the decisions that are required to be made can be worked out as objectively as possible. The end result should be more effective performance on the part of any organization.

The general systems approach is thus not a new theory of how businesses or public bodies should function. It is not a brand-new idea sprung recently from some lofty mind which proper marketing might sell to businessmen. The systems approach, in essence, has been used by businessmen and other managers for many years. A substantial body of data on how it operates has accumulated. The collection of these data over the past decades and the development of machines to process data swiftly and come up with answers, has brought the systems approach into prominence today.

What we are saying is that it is now possible to look scientifically at such a complicated thing as a business. It is now possible to do some analysis of the parts and interactions in a business and help run the business in a more effective manner. This was never possible before, due to lack of tools, essentially, as well as lack of data.

The dictionaries describe a system as a set of complicated things or parts that are interconnected. Herbert Simon, well-known researcher in organization and author of *The New Science of Decision Making,* * stated at a special seminar of experts in management theory and research held years ago at the University of California:

> The term "systems," therefore, does not denote an approach to management theory that is antithetical to, or even distinct from, empirical observation, development of behavioral theories, use of a decision-making frame of analysis, or application of mathematical techniques. It denotes a concern, in the conduct of all these activities, with complexity and with the necessity for developing tools that are especially adapted to handling complexity. No one who has observed closely the developments of the past decade can avoid, I think, the optimistic conclusion that we now have some powerful tools of this kind, and the promise of more.†

*New York: Harper & Row, 1960.
†Harold Koontz, ed., *Toward a Unified Theory of Management* (New York: McGraw-Hill, 1964), pp. 84–85.

Now it is possible to understand more fully all the aspects of management and how they are integrated. This does not mean that we know all there is to know about how the organization works as a system. Far from it. There is a long way to go before we ever—if this is even possible—can fully comprehend the complexities of any organization and have it in perfect dynamic balance with its environment. Setting objectives, changing objectives, devising strategies, changing strategies, making working together more creative (and this does not mean devoid of conflict at all)—these and many more things will constitute the work of managers. The systems approach will give each manager a better way to tackle the problems of management. It does not cut down work, it only cuts out useless work. It is not a panacea, it is a planned approach.

The General Systems Idea

Let us look at what is meant by general systems theory and where an organization fits in the scheme of things. Then we will examine this latter part more closely in order to see the application to organization thinking and where some of the functions such as directing, controlling, and planning fit.

Much of the early work in this area was done by Ludwig von Bertalanffy, a biologist, and Kenneth Boulding, an economist who became very interested in the overall functions of an organization. However, general systems theory is not restricted to business or other organizations but represents a broad scientific way of looking at things.

Briefly, the various levels of systems in our world are as follows:

Level 1: a static structure or framework. The geography and physical structure of our world is one example.

Level 2: a basically mechanical system with predetermined activities. A mechanical clock fits this description, as does the solar system.

Level 3: a basically mechanical system with a built-in control mechanism to make alterations when required. The heat control system in most houses is a good example.

Level 4: a so-called "open" system, which seems to have a "will" of its own. This is the start of a life system in contrast to previous dead systems. A simple cell is a good example.

Level 5: a stage beyond the open system, with genetic factors reacting to the environment. A plant is an example.

Level 6: the system begins to have some awareness of its own and develops special items such as eyes and ears and a brain and nervous system. An animal fits in here.

Level 7: this brings us to the level of people, where there is a consciousness beyond the simple level of awareness.

We go on to more levels. An organization which is composed of people could be said to constitute a level of its own. We might even go on to a system level involving unknown forces. We are beginning to make conscious some of these now, but presumably there will always be questions man cannot answer, so we might as well put these items into a ninth level.

The basic reason for showing these levels is to demonstrate that there are various levels of structure in our world. As we study complicated systems such as that of an organization, we cannot back away from trying to understand it because it is not a simple system such as we are used to. Doing this has led to a laissez-faire attitude toward organization and, therefore, toward management itself. This book has been concerned with dealing with a structured approach, but not with a *mechanical* one. Knowing the structure is the basis for practicing management skills. As we have pointed out several times, it is not the be all and end all. It is the start and should not be swept away by a complete gut-feeling approach. The systems approach shows that there is structure all around us at various levels and that we can place an organization into this scheme of things.

Where an Organization Fits

The organization, as we have noted, is an open system in balance with its environment—economic, political, social, competitive, and so on. This is never a steady balance, always a changing one. Some of the early management science protagonists used to think of an organization as a second-level system, that is, a clockwork one. This view was helpful up to a point, but hardly sophisticated enough to express reality today. An organization is also composed of subsystems, including marketing, production, and many others.

You can already see the vital importance of proper information and communications within the total system if integration is to function smoothly. You can also see that there can be difficulties in defining the boundaries of any subsystem as well as the actual boundary of the organization itself, considered as a whole. An organization functions in an environment. Make-or-buy decisions are a reflection of the problem of where to draw the boundaries. But it can go beyond that.

Let us look at the scientific approach to the study of a system. This is the approach used whether the system being studied is economic, biological, or astronomical. We study what goes into the system and what comes out of it, being careful to see real causes and effects in a social system, such as a business. Social analysis can be tricky, but it should be carried on in this systems manner if we are to avoid simplistic, mechanical conclusions. As data are accumulated, hopefully mainly by observing real-life situations in organizations, we begin to get some understanding of what goes on. After a time we obtain some ideas of the underlying patterns of the system and forces at work within it. The more we get to know, the better become our checks and observations, and the more knowledge we obtain of our original unknown.

This work involves many, many observations. It is not just a simple look. Because social and biological systems are extremely complicated, it was hard to analyze and understand a complete system, and we often had to be content to obtain knowledge of some parts of it. Computers, which can handle vast amounts of information, have made it possible to sort out the workings of a complicated system. This has also helped simplify some of the thinking.

A More Complicated Look

Figure 9 shows a more complicated "systems" picture of an organization. The first point to observe is that the system functions ac-

Figure 9. Step one in a systems view of an organization.

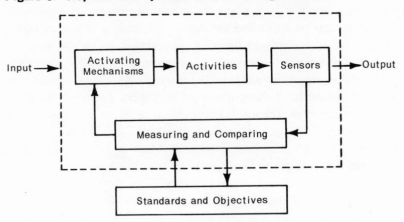

cording to standards and objectives. These must be set down, and there must be a plan to carry them out. The sensors check to see if things are going all right by measuring output—for example, physical measures or return on investment (or both) and many more. The information received is checked against desirable standards—whether these be inventory levels, or 10 percent return, or whatever—and communicated to the activating mechanism. This leads to necessary corrections. This is feedback operating in the system.

All these activities are not necessarily machine-operated and machine-controlled. People still work in tandem with machines, on assembly lines as well as in management areas. Producing a return on the dollar invested still has to be done by people. Any organization operates on a combination of human and machine activities, though more and more of checking and controlling can be carried out by machines these days. Organizations are employing little automatic systems in more and more areas of their activities. We now see a system as having:

- A collection of parts
- Relationships between the parts as well as within them
- Inputs and outputs
- Measures of effectiveness

Furthermore, the system operates in an environment.

We have already used some well-known management terms here, such as objectives, plans, and controls. We see that the system must have structure and the parts must be related to each other in order for the whole to function properly. It should be obvious that the proper information must flow from part to part so that all points where decisions are being made, the requisite information is available. Above all there must be intelligent goals and rational plans for achieving them.

Behind Controls

When we examine the meaning of controls, which involve measuring output, checking it against standards, and then taking any action if necessary to change the processing operations, we discover that a number of vital points have to be considered before we can make use of controls.

One, we must know what to measure and control, because clearly we cannot control everything. The key factors controlled must be those which are most important to ensuring the desired output. The success of the system depends on the selection of these key factors.

Two, we must be able to measure the factors selected. If we choose, for example, the creativity of an engineering section as an item to be measured, then how do we measure this? This does not mean it cannot be measured, but we must have useful ways of doing this.

Three, we must have standards to compare our measurements with so that we can check if the system is operating properly.

Four—tied in with the third item—there must be known ways of making corrections to put the system back in proper operation; otherwise there is no point in selecting items to be measured in the first place. This fourth item really consists of two parts: (1) the relaying of the necessary information to the men or machines in charge and of the corrective actions necessary to get back on the track, and (2) the provision of the means by which the men and/or machines may institute these actions.

The systems approach is by no means a "fun" approach which calls for no work on the part of managers. In setting up systems or subsystems, a tremendous amount of work is involved. This may lead to the elimination of some of the thinking required by clerical workers or many middle managers, but it does not eliminate a lot of slugging. When subsystems can be programmed as the result of this work, then a system may operate without human interference, and people will be called on to use their brains only in nonprogrammed activities and in rechecking programmed ones to make them more effective.

If we introduce all of our older terms, such as planning, controlling, and directing, into a systems diagram, we will have something like Figure 10. Here we have what we have called the functions of management melded into the systems concept. The benefit of this new concept is to help us understand the relationships better and to provide a basis for creating a more effective structure, one which will develop a proper flow of the proper information so that the most effective type of decisions can be made, leading the organization dynamically along the path set out by *objectives*.

Figure 10. Systems flow chart of management of an organization.

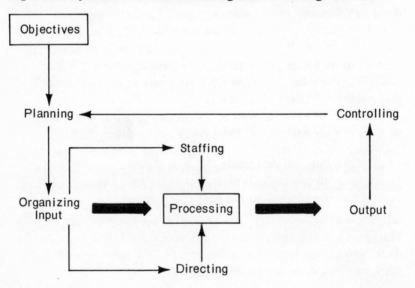

The approach also demonstrates the need for an effective performance on the part of the whole, and shows that this is not necessarily the sum total of optimal performances by the subsystems.

Questions for Review

1. What are the main reasons for setting up controls? How do you approach the problems in setting them up?

_____

_____

_____

_____

_____

_____

_____

_____

2. You are undertaking a project that consists of 10 interconnected and interdependent events. We will call them events A, B, C, D, E, F, G, H, I, J. A is the starting point and J the final event. For the events that are interconnected, here are the times to go from one to another:

A to B: 5 days	A to C: 4 days	B to D: 6 days
B to E: 4 days	C to E: 3 days	C to F: 6 days
B to G: 13 days	D to G: 4 days	E to J: 12 days
F to H: 5 days	F to I: 4 days	I to H: 3 days
H to J: 3 days	G to H: 4 days	

Set up a diagram and determine the critical path (see Chapter 3 on the critical path method). Which events, as now organized, might create difficulties if you do not plan in advance?

Index